history a

THE MAKING OF MODERN ITALY
1800-71

Vyvyen Brendon

Hodder & Stoughton

A MEMBER OF THE HODDER HEADLINE GROUP

ACKNOWLEDGEMENTS

Cover – *Tuscan Troops Saluted at Montechiaro by French Troops Wounded at Solferino*, reproduced courtesy of AKG Photo, London; Foto Scala, Firenze p.14; Bibliothèque Nationale de France p.22; Index, Firenze p.39, 88, 99, 102; The British Library Newspaper Library p.45; Civica Raccolta delle Stampe Achille Bertarelli – Castello Sforzesco – Milano pp.51, 112; Museo Nazionale del Risorgimento Italiano di Torino p.107; The Royal Archives © Her Majesty The Queen p.73; Life File p.119.

Text acknowledgements on page iv

Every effort has been made to trace and acknowledge ownership of copyright. The publishers will be glad to make suitable arrangements with any copyright holders whom it has not been possible to contact.

Author's Acknowledgements

I am grateful to Carolyn Cooksey of St. Mary's School, Cambridge for her interest, encouragement and help.

Order queries: please contact Bookpoint Ltd, 39 Milton Park, Abingdon, Oxon OX14 4TD. Telephone: (44) 01235 400414, Fax: (44) 01235 400454. Lines are open from 9.00–6.00, Monday to Saturday with a 24 hour message answering service. Email address: orders@bookpoint.co.uk

British Library Cataloguing in Publication Data
A catalogue record for this title is available from The British Library

ISBN 0 340 688 416

First published 1998
Impression number 10 9 8 7 6 5 4 3 2 1
Year   2002 2001 2000 1999 1998

Copyright © 1998 Vyvyen Brendon

All rights reserved. No part of this publication may be reproduced or transmitted in any form or by any means, electronic or mechanical, including photocopy, recording, or any information storage and retrieval system, without permission in writing from the publisher or under licence from the Copyright Licensing Agency Limited. Further details of such licences (for reprographic reproduction) may be obtained from the Copyright Licensing Agency Limited of 90 Tottenham Court Road, London W1P 9HE.

Typeset by Fakenham Photosetting Limited, Fakenham, Norfolk NR21 8NL
Printed in Great Britain for Hodder & Stoughton Educational, a division of Hodder Headline Plc, 338 Euston Road, London NW1 3BH by Redwood Books, Trowbridge, Wilts

CONTENTS

Approaching Source-based Questions		1
Introduction		2
1	Alfieri and the People of Italy	7
2	Napoleon Bonaparte and the 'Liberation' of Italy: 1796–1815	17
3	Metternich and the Repression of Italy: 1815–31	29
4	Mazzini and Dreams of a United Italy: 1831–47	41
5	Charles Albert and *Italia Farà da Sé*: 1848–9	54
6	Cavour and the Leadership of Italy: 1849–58	67
7	Napoleon III and the Uniting of Northern Italy: 1859–60	79
8	Garibaldi and the Liberation of the South: 1860	91
9	Bismarck, Pius IX and the Inclusion of Venice and Rome: 1861–71	104
10	Who United Italy?	117
11	Dealing with Examination Questions	127
	Specimen Answers to Source-based Questions	127
	Preparing Essay Answers	130
	Possible Essay Titles	131
	Specimen Essay Answer	134
Bibliography		137
Index		139
Glossary of Foreign Terms		140

TEXT ACKNOWLEDGEMENTS

The publishers would like to thank the following for their permission to reproduce material in this volume.

Cambridge University Press for the extract from *Cavour and Garibaldi* (1985); Economica, Paris for the extracts from *Magenta et Solferino* by R. Bougerie (1993); Eyre and Spottiswoode for the extract from *Pio Nono* by E. E. Yales (1954); John Calder for the extract from *Rome, Naples and Florence in 1817* by C. Stendhal (translated by R. Coe); Laurence and Wishart for the extract from *Prison Notebooks* (edited by Q. Hoare and G. Nowell Smith, 1971); Macmillan for the extract from *The Napoleonic Empire* by G. Ellis (1991); Methuen for the extract from *A History of Italy 1700–1860: The Social Constraints of Political Change* by S. Woolf (1979); Oxford University Press for the extracts from *Makers of Modern Italy: Napoleon to Mussolini* by J. A. L. Mariott (1931), *Victor Emmanuel, Cavour and the Risorgimento* by D. Mack Smith (1971), *Things I Remember* by M. d'Azeglio (translated by E. R. Vincent), *My Prisons* by S. Pellico (translated by G. Capaldi, 1963), *The Diary of One of Garibaldi's Thousand* (translated by E. R. Vincent, 1962); Penguin for the extract from *The Prince* by J. N. Machiavelli (translated by G. Bull, 1961) and for the extract from *The Charterhouse of Parma* by Stendhal (1958); Routledge for the extract from *The Italian Risorgimento* by L. Riall (1994); Sempringham Publishing for the extract from the article in *New Perspective* entitled 'Myth and Reality in the Risorgimento' by B. Haddock (December, 1996); Thomas Nelson for the extract from *Nationmaking in Nineteenth-Century Europe* by W. Shreeves (1984); Yale University Press for the extract from *Mazzini* by D. Mack Smith (1994); the extract from N. Rodolico's review (1960) of D. Mack Smith's 'Italy: a Modern History' (1959) which appeared in *The Risorgimento and the Unification of Italy* by D. Beales (Longman, 1981) and the extract from *History of the Fascist Movement* by G. Volpe (Milan, 1933) which appeared in *The Italian Risorgimento* by S. Woolf (Longman, 1969).

Every effort has been made to trace and acknowledge ownership of copyright. The publishers will be glad to make suitable arrangements with any copyright holders whom it has not been possible to contact.

APPROACHING SOURCE-BASED QUESTIONS

This book aims to provide a set of key documents illustrating the unification of Italy between 1796 and 1870, and to suggest how the material can best be analysed and interpreted. Questions based on documents form a compulsory part of all A level history exam papers. Some boards include documentary questions in outline courses and all make them a dominant feature of depth studies. It is not unusual for as much as 50 per cent of the marks to be allocated to the document section. The questions vary; some require the study of prescribed texts, extracts from which appear on the exam paper for analysis. Others do not indicate specific texts but set detailed questions on documentary extracts that might not have been seen previously, but which candidates should be able to analyse in the light of their contextual knowledge.

Some questions test the candidates' ability to read and understand a historical document. Others examine background knowledge of wider themes or probe understanding of special topics. The most demanding are those which ask for evaluation of a source.

All papers indicate the marks on offer. These are a guide to the relative importance of the question and the proportion of time to be spent on it. As a rough rule of thumb, each mark should correspond to a point of fact or analysis. This should not be followed slavishly however; candidates can waste valuable time trying to find an extra point merely to satisfy an apparent numerical requirement.

Care should be taken to deal with the question as set. Examinees asked to evaluate a document will gain little from paraphrasing it or giving irrelevant details about its background. As well as showing understanding of sources, candidates at this level are expected to have an appreciation of historiography; that is, to know something about the problems in writing history. Being able to spot bias, attitude and motive in the writer of an extract is important. Questions requiring comment on the 'tone' of a passage are common. In responding to such questions candidates should ask themselves whether the writer seems angry, bitter, confident, detached or involved. Does the extract suggest that the source was written for a particular audience or is it a personal statement? Is it propaganda or objective reporting? If candidates train themselves to do this, they will develop analytical skills that merit high marks. Such an appreciation of historical material will also help examinees a great deal in their handling of essay titles.

INTRODUCTION

On 12 May 1997 a group of Venetian 'independence fighters' occupied the bell tower in St Mark's Square, Venice. Displaying an acute sense of history, they staged their action on the 200th anniversary of Napoleon I's conquest of the ancient Venetian Republic – though this cannot be said to have helped their ill-fated bid to separate Venice from Italy.

The city was unusual in having a republican form of government during the 1790s. Its neighbour, Lombardy, lay within the Austrian Empire and the rest of Italy consisted of separate states, ruled by autocratic kings and dukes (mostly of foreign extraction) or by the Pope. The political divisions of the peninsula seemed as immovable as the Apennine mountain range which bisects it. [Chapter 1]

However, Napoleon managed to march over both mountains and frontiers and to recreate Italy in his own image. This was initially republican but (after 1804) imperial. At first Italian nationalists welcomed the French as liberators who would bring constitutional government and unity to their land. But it was not long before French plunder, taxes and conscription aroused widespread resentment. [Chapter 2]

Once Napoleon had been defeated – the achievement of the Great Powers, not of the Italian people – most of the old 'legitimate' rulers were restored by the Treaty of Vienna of 1815. The Venetian Republic was not revived, however, and this region became part of an enlarged Austrian empire. In fact, Austria now dominated Italy. Attempts in 1820 and 1831 to challenge the settlement by establishing more liberal regimes were crushed by Austrian troops. [Chapter 3]

In spite of repression (and partly in response to it) the idea of a free, united Italy grew in the 1830s and 1840s. The exiled revolutionary, Guiseppe Mazzini, never tired in his efforts to convince Italians that their destiny was to be citizens of a democratic republic. More conservative writers proposed a federation led by the Pope or by the strongest Italian state, the Kingdom of Piedmont. But all their books and pamphlets had to be published outside Italy, where even the suggestion of a common railway system was considered dangerous. Nationalist ideas could be legitimately expressed at this time only in the more veiled forms of literature and opera. [Chapter 4]

The year 1848 brought a brief liberal spring to Italy as to other parts of Europe. The new Pope, Pius IX, introduced reforms in the Papal States. Charles Albert of Piedmont turned himself into a constitutional monarch

Introduction

and led his troops into battle against Austria. Venice freed itself from Austrian rule and proclaimed a new republic. Other rulers granted constitutions. This seemed to be the *risorgimento* [national revival] for which Mazzini and others had yearned. But by the summer most of these triumphs had been reversed, though the besieged Venetian Republic survived for another year. In 1849 nationalist hopes were raised again when a republic was established in Rome under the leadership of Mazzini but this was soon defeated by French troops in response to the Pope's plea for help. By then Charles Albert had abdicated after failing in a second bid for Italian independence. His successor, Victor Emmanuel II, retained his father's constitution. It was all that remained of the year of revolutions. [Chapter 5]

During the 1850s more realistic steps towards Italian liberation were taken in Piedmont. Its clever new Prime Minister, Camillo Cavour, first built up the economic strength of the kingdom and then sought an ally with whom to resume the fight against Austria. He courted Napoleon III, Emperor of France, first at the Paris Conference ending the Crimean War (in which Piedmontese soldiers had fought beside the French) and then in a secret meeting at the spa town of Plombières. In 1858 the two leaders made an agreement which suited the interests of both their countries. [Chapter 6]

This took effect in 1859 when the planned war broke out. But Cavour's schemes were thwarted when, after two decisive French victories in Lombardy, the unpredictable emperor signed an early truce which left Austria in possession of Venice. Even so, both France and Piedmont gained from a further deal struck in March 1860. The border provinces of Savoy and Nice were handed over to France in return for her recognition of an enlarged Piedmont. This comprised not only Lombardy but also the central duchies and part of the Papal States, where there had been successful revolutions. A third of Italy had thus been unified, though many nationalists felt that a true *risorgimento* should not have had to depend on foreign help. [Chapter 7]

One malcontent was the patriot-soldier, Guiseppe Garibaldi, whose volunteer army had fought in the wars of 1848–9 and 1859. Now he mourned the loss of Savoy and Nice and determined to liberate the rest of the peninsula. In May 1860 he and his famous Thousand sailed for Sicily where he was greeted as a saviour. Popular support, as well as his own military prowess, enabled Garibaldi to defeat the Bourbon regime in Sicily and Naples by September. His intention was also to gain Rome, which nationalists saw as the destined capital of Italy. But the cautious Cavour, fearing that this would cause conflict with the French troops which still protected the Pope, sent the Piedmontese army to forestall any attack on the Holy City. Garibaldi then decided to hand over his conquests to King Victor Emmanuel, which made a united Italy possible. The new Kingdom was proclaimed in March 1861 – but it did not include Venice or Rome. [Chapter 8]

Despite several valiant attempts by the Garibaldini neither city was gained by Italian efforts. Rather, both fell to Italy through the actions of the Prussian Chancellor, Bismarck. Venice was handed over in the aftermath of Austria's defeat in the Austro-Prussian war of 1866. And the Pope gave up Rome only when French troops were withdrawn to fight Prussia in 1870. Though both Venetians and Romans voted to become part of Italy they were disappointed not to have won freedom for themselves. [Chapter 9]

Italians usually refer to the creation of their country as the Risorgimento and every Italian city now contains streets named after its 'heroes': Mazzini, Garibaldi, Cavour and Victor Emmanuel II. Monuments and museums, as well as history books, have also tended to emphasise their contribution to the making of Italy. In recent years, however, historians have focused on less heroic factors such as foreign intervention, diplomacy, rivalry, opportunism and sheer chance. Moreover, at a time when separatism is growing in Italy, it is suggested that the process of unification took too little account of social problems and regional loyalties. In their attempt to reverse history, the occupants of the Venetian bell-tower drew attention to a debate which has yet to be resolved. [Chapter 10]

Chronology of the Unification of Italy

1796	Invasion of Italy by Napoleon Bonaparte and conquest of Piedmont, Lombardy, Papal States and central duchies
1797	Conquest of Venetian Republic
	Creation of Cisalpine and Ligurian Republics
1798	Cession of Venetia to Austria in Treaty of Campo Formio
1799	Creation of Roman and Neapolitan Republics
	French annexation of Piedmont
	Expulsion of French from Italy by Austria and Russia
1800	Second invasion by Napoleon and victory at Marengo
	Creation of North Italian Republic
1805	Napoleon crowned King of Italy in Milan
1806	Joseph Bonaparte crowned King of Naples
1807	Milan Decree to strengthen Continental System
1808	Marshal Murat made King of Naples
1809	Expulsion of Pope from Rome
1813	Defeat of Napoleon at Leipzig (Battle of the Nations)
1815	Napoleon's escape from Elba and Murat's attempted rising
	Treaty of Vienna: return of most previous rulers

Introduction

1820		Revolutions in Naples, Sicily and Piedmont
1821		Crushing of revolutions by Austrian troops
1831		Revolutions in central Italy defeated by Austrian army
		Founding of Young Italy by Mazzini at Marseilles
1832		Publication of Pellico's *My Prisons*
1839		Beginning of scientific congresses
1841		Composition of Verdi's *Nabucco*
1842		Rewriting in Italian of Manzoni's *The Betrothed*
1843		Publication of Gioberti's *Primato*
1844		Publication of Balbo's *Hopes of Italy*
		Attempted revolution in Calabria by Bandiera brothers
1846		Inauguration of Pope Pius IX
1847		Founding of *Il Risorgimento* by Cavour and Balbo
1848	*January*	Revolution in Kingdom of Naples and Sicily
	March	New constitution in Piedmont
		Revolution in Lombardy and Austrian withdrawal
		Revolution in Venice and Austrian withdrawal
		Declaration of war on Austria by Charles Albert
	April	Pope's condemnation of war
	May	Restoration of royal power in Naples
	July	Defeat of Charles Albert at Custoza and armistice
		Austrian reoccupation of Lombardy
1849	*February*	Declaration of Roman Republic
	March	Piedmont's renewal of war and defeat at Novara
		Charles Albert's abdication and accession of Victor Emmanuel II
	April	Arrival of French army outside Rome
	June	Defeat of Roman Republic and restoration of Pope
	August	Defeat of Venetian Republic by Austria
1852		Appointment of Cavour as Prime Minister of Piedmont
1854		Piedmont's participation in Crimean War
1856		Italian question raised at Paris Peace Conference
		Founding of National Society in Turin
1857		Death of Pisacane in attempted rising at Naples
1858		Attempt on Napoleon III's life by Orsini in Paris
		Plombières agreement between Cavour and Napoleon III
1859	*April*	Outbreak of war between France and Austria
		Revolution in Tuscany and establishment of provisional government
	May	Revolutions in Parma, Modena and Romagna
	June	French victories at Magenta and Solferino
	July	Peace of Villafranca and resignation of Cavour
1860	*January*	Cavour's return to office

The Making of Modern Italy

	March	Plebiscites in Tuscany, Parma, Modena and Romagna in favour of annexation by Piedmont
	April	Plebiscites in Savoy and Nice in favour of annexation by France
		Departure of Garibaldi's expedition to Sicily
	May	Conquest of Sicily by Garibaldi
	August	Garibaldi's invasion of mainland
	September	Garibaldi's entry into Naples and victory at Volturno
		Piedmontese invasion of Papal States
	October	Plebiscites in Naples, Sicily and Papal States in favour of union with Piedmont
1861		Elections for Italian Parliament and declaration of Victor Emmanuel as King of Italy
		Beginning of civil war in southern Italy
		Death of Cavour
1862		Garibaldi's attempted march on Rome halted at Aspromonte
1864	*September*	Convention between Italy and Napoleon III
		Pope's *Syllabus of Errors*
1866		Alliance between Italy and Prussia and neutrality agreement between France and Austria
		Defeat of Italian troops during Austro-Prussian war
		Failed Italian naval attack at Lissa
		Cession of Venetia to Italy by France
		Italian capital moved to Florence
1867		Defeat of Garibaldi's attempted invasion of Rome
1870		Outbreak of Franco-Prussian war and removal of French troops from Rome
		Declaration of Papal Infallibility
		Declaration of Rome as capital of Italy
1871		Law of Guarantees leaves Pope with Vatican

1 ALFIERI AND THE PEOPLE OF ITALY

In 1792 the writer, Vittorio Alfieri, ran into difficulties as he was trying to cross the French frontier into his native Piedmont. Desperate to convince officials that he was not a French aristocrat escaping from the Revolution, he shouted, 'Look, Listen! Alfieri is my name! I am an Italian, not a Frenchman!' Such a statement was unusual since in those days most inhabitants of this distinctive peninsula, so clearly defined by the Alps and the Mediterranean, did not think of themselves as Italian. This is hardly surprising: Italians were divided from each other by a host of factors, geographical, economic, social, linguistic and political.

The peninsula is divided along the whole of its length by the high Apennine range and about four-fifths of the land consists of mountains. The hilly islands of Sicily and Sardinia are clearly cut off from mainland Italy. Less obvious is the disparity between the temperate river valleys of the north and the arid Mediterranean landscape of the south. [A]

In these various environments people lived in very different ways. In the plains of the river Po and the foothills of the Alps busy rentier-farmers produced vines, rice, maize, flax, Gorgonzola cheese and the mulberries on which the important silk industry was based. The sharecropping peasants of central Italy were poorer and more backward, but market-gardeners and fruit-growers made a better living around cities like Florence and Bologna. Shepherds herded their flocks in the mountains of the Abruzzi and Apulia. Roman, Neapolitan and Sicilian landowners grew cash crops like tobacco and wheat on their vast estates [*latifundia*], while the peasants of these regions lived mainly on maize and beans and had to resort to grass and seeds in time of famine. [B–D]

Most Italians at this time were illiterate but even those who had had some education found it difficult to communicate with people from other regions. French was spoken in Piedmont and the popes insisted on the official use of Latin in the Papal States. The Spanish Bourbon regime in the south and the Austrian Habsburg rulers in the north had introduced their own languages. In addition regional dialects were virtually different tongues, often incomprehensible to both Italian and foreign travellers. Alfieri was very aware of these linguistic variations. He grew up speaking French in his noble Piedmontese household, thought that the local 'jargon' was 'ill calculated' to improve his Italian style and decided to 'defrenchify' himself by going to Tuscany where 'real Italian' was spoken. He first had to beg the King for permission to leave Piedmont: 'It was necessary that I should bend myself very low, but happily this did not prevent me from afterwards assuming my upright stance.' As this experience suggests, the Italian peninsula consisted of separate, autonomous, rival states. [E–F]

Alfieri's native land was the independent Kingdom of Piedmont, which included the island of Sardinia and the trans-alpine provinces, Savoy and Nice. It was ruled autocratically by the House of Savoy, represented by King Victor Amadeus III. Among the repressive measures imposed by this regime was the censorship of all writing, which led the young Alfieri to renounce his citizenship in 1778: 'I could not be both a subject *and* an author. I chose the latter.' He could not have predicted the leading role which Piedmont was to play in the unification of Italy. Yet its possession of a strong army and an effective bureaucracy already marked this kingdom out as a potential leader among Italian states.

Piedmont's neighbour, Lombardy, was part of the Austrian Empire. The last two Habsburg Emperors, Joseph II and Leopold II, had been enlightened despots, who had modernised the state and reduced the power of the Church. But in spite of these changes Italians did not play a significant role in government, an exclusion which some found frustrating. The remaining areas of northern Italy formed the ancient republics of Venice and Genoa. Both had long and proud histories but by this time they were decadent states governed by small groups of privileged noblemen.

Further south there were various duchies, most of whose dukes were not Italian. The Grand Dukes of Tuscany were Habsburgs, who ruled in a tolerant and benevolent fashion. The Duchy of Parma and Piacenza was governed by Spanish Bourbons. Only Modena and its tiny neighbouring states were controlled by Italian dynasties. [G]

Also in central Italy, straddling the Apennines, were the extensive lands over which the popes held sway. Despite his name, Pius VI (1775–1800) was not a particularly pious man, but he made some efforts to improve the well-being of his impoverished subjects.

Even more miserable conditions prevailed in the large southern Kingdom of the Two Sicilies. It was ruled by Ferdinand I (1760–1825) of the Spanish Bourbon family, an ill-educated man dominated by his Austrian wife Caroline who was influenced in turn by her English 'favourite' and minister, John Acton. This foreign court resided at Naples and was represented in Sicily by viceroys, some of whom had introduced limited reforms. In both parts of the kingdom most of its subjects suffered from acute poverty, which they blamed principally on the enclosure of common land. It also angered them that the state maintained a large army and that the Church enjoyed an enormous income, as did many landowners. [H]

Thus there was little to connect the states of the Italian peninsula, which vied with each other for territory. Even people lucky enough to be granted a passport found it difficult to travel from one to another since communications were so poor. Nevertheless it is possible to discern some factors which gave some prospect of a united Italy.

It was Italy's famous past which inspired Alfieri to long for a *risorgimento*. [L] In classical times Rome had been the centre of an empire stretching from Hadrian's Wall to the first cataract of the Nile. Even after the Roman Empire collapsed and the peninsula was divided among 'barbarian' invaders, individual city states like Florence, Milan and Venice dominated European trade and banking. In the fifteenth century their wealthy rulers patronised artists like Leonardo da Vinci and Michelangelo and fostered that rebirth of learning known as the Renaissance (whose art and architecture attracted tourists in the eighteenth and nineteenth centuries just as they do today). Educated Italians were also proud of the fine Tuscan language, used by Dante and Machiavelli. Furthermore, the Papacy had for centuries given Italy international importance as well as religious uniformity. [I–J]

There were also more modern factors making for unity. In the late eighteenth century the relatively enlightened governments of states like Tuscany and Lombardy gave some educated Italians a new optimism.[K] The recent phenomenon of capitalist growth, small-scale though it was, was beginning to demonstrate the advantages of becoming a single country where internal frontiers would not impede trade and communications. Outside influences also played their part. According to some contemporaries and historians the 'evil germ' of Italian nationalism, as Metternich called it, was incubated in revolutionary France. Alfieri himself rejected the French 'demagogues of the day' as 'worshippers of a false liberty'. Other Italians longed for revolution in Italy and welcomed the Napoleonic armies who came to 'liberate' them in 1796.

The Making of Modern Italy

A   A map illustrating the geographical and political divisions of Italy (1815) and showing places mentioned throughout the book

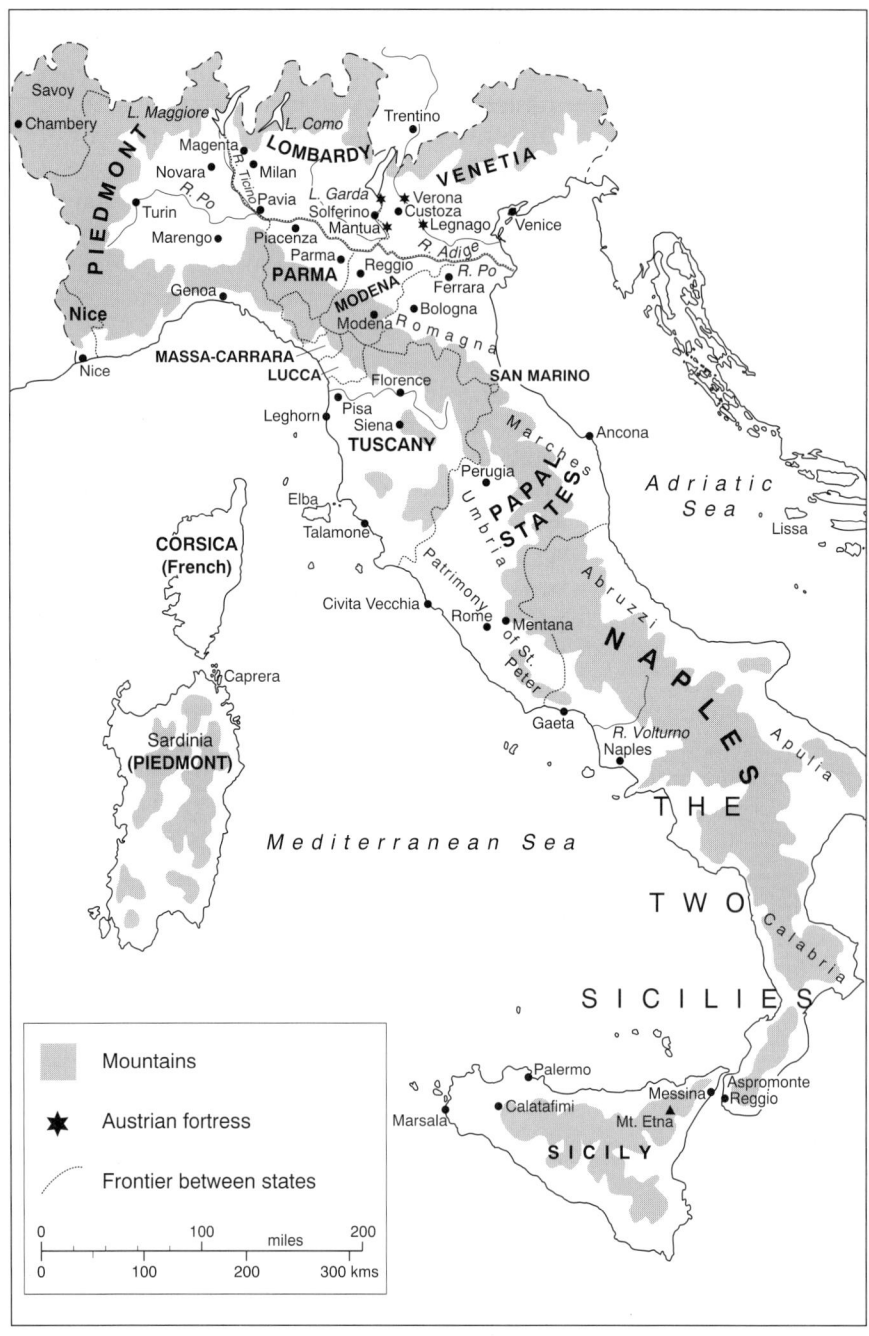

B Liberal Lombard writer, Carlo Ravizza, depicts an old farmer who delights in showing off the improvements he has made

Waste places changed into green and extensive meadows, watery marshes converted into perennial runnels, costly edifices of stone supporting the irrigation canals, granaries full to bursting, the immense hay-barns, the stables of great horses and vigorous oxen. ... However, in spite of the urban luxury brought to the great families of the Plain, Signor Carlo Siro had remained faithful to the old ways, except that he had substituted a fine carriage for the dusty one-horse shay in which his father had visited the markets, and had taken care to have his sons instructed in the colleges and at the University.

From *A Country Priest* by Carlo Ravizza (1841)

C The French writer, Stendhal, describes the view from the city of Florence

If you mount the southern hillside, climbing through the gardens of the *Palazzo Pitti* and from thence embarking upon a circuit of the walls as far as the highroad to Arezzo, you may gain some notion of the countless multitude of little hills which compose the domain of Tuscany; carpeted with olive-groves, with vineyards and with narrow strips of cereal, the undulating surface of the land is cultivated like a garden. And indeed, agriculture is a pursuit most admirably suited to the placid, pacific, husbanding genius of the Tuscan race. The landscape – just as we may observe it in the paintings by Leonardo or by Raphael – often terminates in a perspective of dark foliage against the clear blue of a cloudless sky.

From *Rome, Naples and Florence in 1817* by Stendhal (1817)

D Frances Trollope, wife of the famous English novelist, gives her impressions of southern Italy

The journey from Rome to Naples presents perhaps as lamentable a picture of civilised life as can well be imagined. I think I may venture to say, that no single trace of happy, well paid industry meets the eye from one end of it to the other. Rags, filth, ignorance, and superstition are the prominent features that meet the observation of the traveller. It is hardly possible, I think, to see a greater difference between the external symptoms of character, and the general *manière d'être* [way of life], than may be observed between the peasants of Tuscany, and those of Naples and the Roman States. The Tuscan peasant has a feeling of honest pride in himself, in his decent garments, in the produce of his labour, and in the roof that his thrift renders comfortable. But of this, there is not a trace left on your journey

The Making of Modern Italy

southward. There is a look of self-abandonment even in the very children, that is terrible.

From *A Visit to Italy* by Mrs Trollope (1842)

E The novelist Alessandro Manzoni explains the difficulties of not having a genuinely national language

Granted that over all Italy there is a common spoken language of a kind. But suppose you have a group of Milanese, not just ordinary people, but well-to-do and educated; and suppose they are talking in the local dialect, as would be the normal custom throughout Italy: then introduce into the circle a Piedmontese, a Bolognese, a Venetian, or a Neapolitan, and watch them give up dialect and try their hand at our common Italian language. Tell me if their conversation goes as before; tell me if those Milanese can touch various subjects with the same richness and sureness of vocabulary. ... The non-Milanese stranger, too, will he not find just the same, that he lacks the full, ready and sure command of speech that he would have at home? And is this really to possess a language in common?

From *The Difficulty of Creating a National Language*, notes by Alessandro Manzoni (c. 1833)

F Italian separateness, as described to Stendhal by Cavaletti, an army officer

Consider the six focal centres of activity which control the destiny of the eighteen million inhabitants of Italy: Turin, Milan, Modena, Florence, Rome and Naples. You do not need telling that these very different peoples are very far from forming a homogeneous nation. Bergamo detests Milan, which is likewise execrated by Novara and Pavia; whereas your Milanese himself, being fully preoccupied with keeping a good table and acquiring a warm overcoat against the winter, hates nobody; for hatred would merely disturb the unruffled serenity of his pleasures. Florence, which in days gone by so bitterly abhorred Siena, now is so reduced to impotence that she has no strength for loathing left; yet, allowing for these two exceptions, I search in vain to discover a third; each city detests its neighbours, and is mortally detested in return. It follows therefore that our rulers have no difficulty in the fulfilment of their aim: *divide ut imperes* [divide in order to rule].

From *Rome, Naples and Florence in 1817* by Stendhal (1817)

G The Piedmontese ambassador to Tuscany recommends to his own conservative sovereign the reforms he has seen operating there

Guided by the soundest principles, he [the Habsburg Duke Leopold who later became Emperor Leopold II] reformed some of the old laws, abolished many others, discontinued many wrongful feudal privileges, suppressed many courts and laid down a very simple, rapid and economical procedure for the judiciary. ... Torture is now abolished in all cases and in every court of Tuscany. Weights and measures were made uniform. ... All the provinces and territories of Tuscany were allowed to organize and administer economic affairs, which previously had been controlled by a few officials in the capital, who were distant, slow, expensive and sometimes open to intrigue and corruption. ... Reform of tariffs and excise duties is in progress. ... The ordered state of the laws and their conscientious and vigilant application has rendered the subjects of Tuscany law-abiding, and assured the peace and safety of the nation.

From a report by Luigi Cotti di Brusaco (1782)

H In an anonymous pamphlet Luigi Settembrini, a southern liberal, blames poverty on successive governments

Our agriculture, which needs government protection and the most assiduous care, comes under a subdepartment run by two or three idiotic clerks. Our land is as fertile as almost anywhere in Italy, but it is deserted, or else is cultivated by a handful of wretched, weary peasants. Immense territories in Sicily, in Calabria, in Abruzzi, in the Principati and even in Apulia are abandoned and malarial. If there is any question of land reclamation, as for instance near the mouth of the Volturno, the Minister gives the job to some personal friend who spends and spends but does nothing. The Minister personally takes some of the land at a light rent and then leases it back to the peasants. If there is an outcry, a Commission is set up whose head is none other than the Minister himself. In such a fertile Kingdom, which could feed double its present population, there is often a bread shortage and people can be found dead of starvation.

From *Protest of the Population of the Two Sicilies* (1847)

The Making of Modern Italy

1 In this early sixteenth-century painting by Ottavio Vannini, *Lorenzo the Magnificent Admiring Michelangelo's Faun*, the Duke of Florence is surrounded by artists who enjoy his patronage. It is typical of the Renaissance in its use of perspective, realistic depiction of people and landscape and inclusion of classical features

Alfieri and the People of Italy

J The sixteenth-century writer, Machiavelli, was revered during the Risorgimento both for his use of the Italian language and for his call to Italians to unite against foreign invasions. In the last chapter of his famous political treatise, *The Prince*, he urges the ruler of Florence to lead this national revival

If the Israelites had to be enslaved in Egypt for Moses to emerge as their leader; if the Persians had to be oppressed by the Medes so that the greatness of Cyrus could be recognized; if the Athenians had to be scattered to demonstrate the excellence of Theseus: then, at the present time, in order to discover the worth of an Italian spirit, Italy had to be brought to her present extremity. ... So now, left lifeless, Italy is waiting to see who can be the one to heal her wounds. ... See how Italy beseeches God to send someone to save her from those barbarous cruelties and outrages; see how eager and willing the country is to follow a banner, if only someone will raise it. And at the present time it is impossible to see in what she can place more hope than in your illustrious House [the Medici family], which ... can lead Italy to her salvation.

From *The Prince* by N. Machiavelli (1513)

K The Milanese writer, Giuseppe Parini, sees hope for the future in more enlightened Austrian rule (this essay was written for the Austrian Minister, Firmian, who was prone to dismiss Italian comments as 'impertinence')

Certainly no one will deny that the suppression of Florentine liberty, the excessive power in Italy of the Spaniards, whose governors cruelly oppressed her most beautiful places, the decline of Venetian greatness ... , the hypocrisy introduced into the papal court after the reforms of Luther [the Protestant leader], and the cruelty of the Inquisition [the Catholic campaign against Protestantism], ... extinguished in Italy all feelings of national glory, of noble rivalry and freedom of thought, with the result that almost all Italians were greatly degraded in spirit. This situation should have enslaved of literature and all fine arts in Italy, and made them mediocre and barbaric. But despite so many evils, the extraordinary genius of a few great men and the example of the past kept alive the seeds of good taste. It would be easy to develop these again, under the present kindly and enlightened government [that of Emperor Joseph II], and so promptly awaken minds and produce excellent works.

From an essay by G. Parini (1773)

The Making of Modern Italy

L   Alfieri was one of the first writers to call for a *risorgimento* in his 'enslaved' country

I do not know whether I am deluding myself, as I was born here: but consideration of the facts shows that this small peninsula is still the same as that which previously conquered nearly all of the then known world, and which nevertheless remained free while conquering – a unique example in history. And it was still the same Italy which a few centuries later enlightened the rest of Europe with the arts and sciences, drawn in fact from Greece, but transmitted across the mountains in a very different form from that in which they had been received from across the sea. And it was still Italy which later civilized the rest of Europe with the divine arts, refashioned rather than imitated by her. And finally it was old, tired, defeated, humiliated Italy, despoiled of all other glories, which still ruled and frightened so many other nations for so long, demanding homage from them by sheer cunning and intelligence. These four ways in which Italy dominated all other countries embrace all human faculties and virtues, and are strong, indubitable proofs that amongst her inhabitants there has always been a very much greater abundance of those fervent spirits who instinctively seek glory in noble deeds – which they achieved to a high degree, albeit differently in different ages.

From *The Prince and Literature* by V. Alfieri (1784)

Questions

1 Compare the tone of the Italian, French and English descriptions of Italy given in sources B–D.   **(5 marks)**
2 What obstacles to Italian unity are illustrated in sources E and F?   **(5 marks)**
3 What can be learnt about the governments of Italy from sources G–H.   **(5 marks)**
4 To what extent do sources I and J justify the pride in Italy's cultural past expressed in source L?   **(5 marks)**
5 Evaluate the reasons for optimism given in sources K and L.   **(5 marks)**

2 NAPOLEON BONAPARTE AND THE 'LIBERATION' OF ITALY: 1796–1815

In May 1796 Napoleon Bonaparte announced to the city of Bologna, which was occupied by French troops under his command: 'The time has come for Italy to take her place with honour among the nations. Lombardy, Bologna, Reggio, Ferrara, perhaps the Romagna, if it shows itself worthy, will one day astonish Europe and re-create the great days of Italy.' The places mentioned by Napoleon were ruled at this time by the Austrian Emperor or the Pope. Was Napoleon sincere in suggesting that he was going to help them to unite and form a nation?

Many Bolognese people had welcomed the French army in the belief that it would enable them to break free from papal rule. Indeed, ever since the outbreak of the French Revolution in 1789, enlightened middle- and upper-class groups in Italian cities had sympathised with French aims: more democratic government, a less powerful church, a more liberal society. Italian governments, on the other hand, had regarded these 'Jacobins' [the French name for revolutionaries] as dangerous and had censored any expression of their ideas. When war broke out in 1792 between revolutionary France and the conservative countries of Europe this enmity became more pronounced. The French Government sent agents to Italy to foment revolution; and several Italian rulers (the Emperor of Austria, the Kings of Piedmont and Naples and the Duke of Tuscany) joined the coalition against France in 1793.

At this point the only parts of Italy 'liberated' by France were the provinces of Savoy and Nice, which had been part of the Kingdom of Piedmont. They were largely French-speaking and had voted for union with France in a plebiscite. Since the acquisition of these areas enabled France to fulfil the aim of expanding to her 'natural frontiers' (in this case the Alps), it is clear that French policy towards Italy was not entirely altruistic.

In 1796 the newly-formed French Directory sought to solve its domestic problems by means of foreign conquest. The brilliant young Corsican, General Napoleon Bonaparte, was given command of France's so-called 'Army of Italy'. (Ironically, Corsica had become French only a year before his birth, so Napoleon narrowly missed being born a citizen of the Republic of Genoa.) Napoleon's army invaded Italy in April and rapidly defeated both the Piedmontese and the Austrian forces despite being outnumbered. In May French troops entered Milan, the capital of Lombardy, and went on to drive the Austrians out of Italy. They also occupied most of the Papal States and the duchies of central Italy. In 1797 they crushed the Venetian Republic. [A–D]

These victories were aided by the presence of Italian Jacobins (calling themselves patriots) who saw the French as liberators. To reward them – and perhaps because he agreed with their aims – Napoleon encouraged the creation of new republics in Italy. The first, in 1796, was the Cispadane Republic which incorporated lands south of the River Po and introduced a constitution drawn up by the patriots of Bologna. But Napoleon dissolved this state a year later because it was too independent, transforming it into the Cisalpine Republic which also included Lombardy. Under Napoleon's aegis the old Republic of Genoa became the Ligurian Republic. He reserved a different fate for Venetia, cynically handing it over to Austria in the Treaty of Campo Formio of 1798. This deal enabled Napoleon to conclude his Italian campaign and seek new conquests in Egypt.

Later in the year the Directory's armies occupied Rome (where a French general had been shot), expelled the Pope and created the Roman Republic. When King Ferdinand of the Two Sicilies (urged on by Admiral Nelson) threatened to re-take Rome, French troops entered Naples in January 1799. After forcing the royal family to flee to Sicily under British naval protection, they proclaimed the Neapolitan Republic. Meanwhile the Piedmontese monarch, who had not proved sufficiently cooperative, had to take refuge in his island province of Sardinia while France annexed the rest of his territory. All of mainland Italy was now under French control.

France clearly gained both security and booty from her 'sister-republics'. It is less clear how well the Italian people fared between 1796 and 1799, a period known in Italy as the *triennio*. Each republic had a constitution resembling that of France, with an elected assembly and an executive consisting of five Directors. Thus Italians participated in government more than they had done before – the Lombards were so excited that they offered a prize for the best essay on 'the free government most suitable to the happiness of Italy'. The new assemblies introduced reforms as radical as those of revolutionary France, abolishing noble titles and privileges, allowing Jews to take part in public life, confiscating and selling off church property. Most Italian liberals approved of these measures. Bourgeois and noble landowners seem on the whole to have gained more (in terms of jobs and land) than they lost; but the peasant majority was more likely to suffer from the changes and to oppose them. [E–G]

The *triennio* ended in 1799 when Austrian and Russian troops ousted the French from northern and central Italy. In Naples Cardinal Ruffo's

Napoleon Bonaparte and the 'Liberation' of Italy: 1796–1815

'Christian and Royal Army', consisting of poor peasants and townsmen, destroyed the six-month-old republic amid scenes of appalling savagery. On the insistence of Admiral Nelson, whose ships had aided this successful counter-revolution, the Jacobin leaders were condemned as traitors. Among the 119 who were executed was Vincenzo Russo who shouted from the scaffold, 'I die for liberty. *Viva la Repubblica!*' In the event, Italy was to enjoy neither liberty nor republicanism over the next fifteen years. [H–J]

At the end of 1799 Napoleon seized political power in France, formed another Army of Italy and crossed the Alps in May the following year. He defeated the Austrians at the crucial battle of Marengo. This enabled him to form a large Italian Republic, of which he was President, and to re-annex Piedmont. After he had crowned himself Emperor of France in 1804, Italy played its part in his imperial designs. By 1806 he had changed the Italian Republic into a kingdom, with himself as King and his stepson Eugene Beauharnais as Viceroy. He had incorporated much of central Italy into the French Empire, and made his brother Joseph King of Naples. As well as making Italy provide army recruits and taxes for his so-called 'Grand Empire', Napoleon made the country cooperate in the Continental Blockade, by which all British goods were to be excluded from Europe. To help enforce this scheme he sent Joseph to rule Spain in 1808 and replaced him as King of Naples with his brother-in-law, Marshal Murat. By now the Italian peninsula was entirely subject to Napoleon and was ruled by the Emperor's principle: *'France first'*. [K]

The French tried to modernise Italy. They abolished internal customs barriers, built canals, bridges and roads, unified weights, measures and currency, abolished censorship (except for works critical of the French Government) and introduced the Napoleonic legal code. They also continued to sell church lands and insist on religious toleration. Recent research suggests that these reforms were not always as significant in practice as they were in theory. In many areas old customs would not die. Elsewhere the changes tended to reinforce current trends, like the enrichment of the bourgeoisie in the north or the consolidation of large estates in the south. Peasants and smallholders seem everywhere to have borne the brunt of rising prices, heavier taxation and relentless conscription.

In its later years Italians increasingly resented Napoleonic rule. There were frequent peasant revolts. Liberal intellectuals and devout churchmen formed rival secret societies opposed to the French. But there was no patriotic Italian rising and Napoleon's empire was brought to an end in 1813 on battlefields far from Italy. One futile revolutionary endeavour was made: in 1815, when Napoleon escaped from his exile on Elba, Murat (who had only kept his throne by siding with Austria and England) tried to raise an army to support him in the name of an independent and united Italy. People did not flock to join this cause and Murat was soon defeated and executed by the Allies – but the call to unity was not forgotten by Italian nationalists. [L]

Italians were left with mixed feelings about Napoleonic domination. Historians too have expressed varied opinions about this extraordinary period. Most agree, however, that although Napoleon did not really intend to 're-create the great days of Italy', his rule did promote the Risorgimento in certain ways. Many educated Italians had gained political or military experience. Frustrated at the loss of these opportunities, some rebelled against their restored rulers after 1815. After all, the Napoleonic era had shown that it was possible to eject old dynasties and to rationalise the political map of Italy. When it was over the Sardinian ambassador to Britain summed up what had been achieved: 'The changes,' he wrote, 'have given a new impetus, a new spirit to our land.' [M–Q]

A The French agent in Italy reports to the Foreign Minister

It is not to be doubted that when our military forces triumph in Piedmont we can rally these local patriots and many others; I believe that in working by a reasonable method to Republicanise the conquered areas in Italy we can obtain advantages, and especially inspire fear and terror in the hearts of all the petty Tyrants by whom this fair country is subjected; but I have never proposed this except as secondary to our victories. ... Let us enter victoriously into Piedmont, the Milanese and all Italy; we shall find a high-spirited people.

From a letter dated 9 April 1796

B General Bonaparte reports to the Directors on his progress through Italy

H.Q. Piacenza, 9 May 1796 At last we have crossed the Po. The second campaign has begun. ... One more victory and we are masters of Italy. ... What we have taken from the enemy is beyond counting. We have hospital equipment for 15,000 sick, several stores of corn, flour etc. The more men you send me, the more easily they can be fed. I am sending you twenty pictures by the greatest masters, by Correggio and Michelangelo. ... If things go well, I hope to be able to send you some 10 million francs to Paris; that should be useful for the Army of the Rhine.

H.Q. Milan, 17 May 1796 The Tricolour flies over Milan, Pavia, Como and all the towns of Lombardy. ... Milan is very eager for liberty; there is a club of 800 members, all businessmen or lawyers. ... We will draw 20 millions in contributions from this country; the land is one of the richest in the universe. ... From here will be sent out the journals and other literature which will set all Italy aflame. If these people ask to set themselves up as a republic, should that be allowed? ... It is a far more patriotic country than Piedmont and is closer to liberty.

From Napoleon's reports during the invasion of Italy, 1796

C The French novelist, Stendhal, gives an ironic account of Milan in 1796

On 15 May 1796, General Bonaparte made his victory into Milan at the head of that youthful army which but a short time before had crossed the Bridge of Lodi, and taught the world that after so many centuries Caesar and Alexander had a successor. ... The departure of the last Austrian regiment marked the collapse of the old ideas; to risk one's life became the fashion. People saw that, in order to be happy after centuries of insipid sensations, they needs must love their country with genuine affection and seek to perform heroic actions. ... Three days after the entry of the French, there were posted up notices of a war levy of six millions, effected for the needs of the French army which, having just won six battles and conquered twenty provinces, wanted nothing now but shoes, breeches, jackets and caps. The vast inrush of happiness and pleasure that poured into Lombardy in the wake of these extremely needy Frenchmen was such that only the priests and a small handful of the nobles were conscious of the heaviness of this levy of six millions, which was shortly after followed by others. The French soldiers laughed and sang the whole day long; they were all under twenty-five years of age, and their Commander-in-Chief, who was twenty-seven, was reckoned the oldest man in his army. This gaiety, this youth, this happy-go-lucky attitude of theirs, provided an amusing answer to the frenzied preaching of the monks who, for six months past, had been proclaiming from the lofty eminence of their pulpits that the French were monsters, obliged, under pain of death, to burn down everything and to cut off everyone's head.

From *The Charterhouse of Parma* by Stendhal (1830)

The Making of Modern Italy

D A French print of 1797 glorifies Napoleon's liberation of Italy

E A Milanese liberal, who became a member of the Provisional Government (the Municipality) set up by the French, tells his brother how he feels about the various changes in 1796

May We are subjects of the invincible French Revolution.
May [after the abolition of titles] Please address your letters to Citizen Verri and not to Count Pietro Verri.
June [after he had been asked to give 30,000 lire and two horses to the French army] The Municipality has allowed itself to become an instrument of the systematic spoliation of our country. Many years,

perhaps a generation, will pass before Milan recovers the luxurious appearance it once had.

August [after censorship was introduced] It is necessary to use the greatest discretion to write to you.

August We are in the position of a people awaiting a Messiah who never comes.

December [after it was clear that the French were going to set up a Republic] Within a few years Italy will probably be a single family. [But Verri died on 28 June 1797, the day before the Cisalpine Republic was established]

From the letters of Pietro Verri

F Napoleon makes sure that the 'independent' republics fit in with his designs

1 May 1797 I have just received news of the Cispadane Republic. Their choice has been very bad. Priests have influenced all the elections. ... I shall start by joining Lombardy and the Cispadane under a single provisional government. Thereafter I shall take steps in harmony with their customs to enlighten opinion and lessen the influence of their priests.

8 May 1797 The choice of members of the Directory of the Cisalpine is pretty bad; it was made in my absence and was completely influenced by the priests. But since Modena and Bologna are to form a single republic with Milan, I have suspended the Government and am having prepared here all the military, civil, financial and administrative laws that must accompany the Constitution. In the first instance I shall myself make all the appointments, and I hope that in three weeks the new Italian Republic will be completely organised and able to stand on its own feet.

From reports by Napoleon to the Directory

G A group of Italian exiles in Paris analyse the reasons for the collapse of the republics set up by the French in Italy

Everybody sincerely welcomed the arrival of the French in Italy, with the exception of inveterate fanatics, arrogant nobles and rascals of all kinds. Even the ignorant people could only talk of the republic, and for the first time interested themselves in the great destiny of the nation. Now things are very different: with the arrival of the enemy, the peoples of Italy either remained indifferent or rose up in revolt against the French troops and the patriots. ... What caused so strange an outcome? ... One of the principal mistakes made in Italy was the complete neglect of the spirit of the nation. A French revolution was organised in the country instead of an Italian one. Even the Italian

The Making of Modern Italy

patriots are guilty of this inconsistency; they spread the ideas, ways, attitudes and even the fantasies of the French Revolution. ... The division of the country into small states is another reason why the public spirit in Italy was not raised as high as possible. Briefly the word Italian would have meant something to all Italians, Lombards, Tuscans, Neapolitans, regardless of origin, while the word Cisalpine has almost no meaning for the Neapolitans etc. ... But Italy can be saved by avoiding these errors the next time. The only way ... is to make Italy into a single republic, closely tied to the French republic by the form of its political constitution and principles.

From *Le Cri d'Italie* (1799)

H   A popular counter-revolutionary rhyme from Naples
Whoever has bread and wine,
Must be a Jacobine

I   Admiral Nelson welcomes strong measures against those who had served in the 'infamous Neapolitan republic'
Palermo, 6 June 1799 to Captain Foote Your news of the hanging of thirteen Jacobins gave us great pleasure; and the three priests will, I hope, return in the *Aurora* to dangle on the tree best adapted to the weight of their sins.
[Later he explains his intervention to the British Government]
Palermo, 13 July 1799 On my fortunate arrival here I found a most infamous treaty entered into with the rebels [which would have allowed them free passage to Toulon], in direct disobedience of his Sicilian Majesty's orders. I had the happiness of saving his Majesty's honour, rejecting with disdain any terms but unconditional submission. ... The rebels came out of the castles with this knowledge, without any honours, and the principal rebels were seized and conducted on board the ships of the squadron. [They were later executed] ... His Majesty has entirely approved of my conduct in this matter.

From the despatches of Lord Nelson

J   A liberal Italian historian takes a different view of the social tensions which caused the bloody end of the Neapolitan Republic
The idealists [i.e. the Jacobins] were a small group of standard-bearers among an ignorant crowd which threatened to, and nearly did overwhelm them, which sent them to prison, death, and exile and inflicted great moral suffering. ... The monarchy ... took fright and had recourse to desperate means of resistance. It ... went over to the opposition, and became definitely negative and reactionary.

From *History of the Kingdom of Naples* by B. Croce (1895)

Napoleon Bonaparte and the 'Liberation' of Italy: 1796–1815

K Napoleon's instructions to his brother Joseph on how to rule Naples are typical of those given to his ruling clan

I see that you promise, in one of your proclamations, not to impose any war taxation; and that you forbid your soldiers to demand full board from their hosts. In my opinion you are adopting measures that are too narrowly conceived. You do not win people to your side by cajoling them, and it is not by measures like these that you will gain the means of providing your army with its rightful recompense. Levy a contribution of thirty millions from the Kingdom of Naples. ... So far as I am concerned, it would be too ridiculous if the conquest of Naples did not bring comfort and well-being to my army. ... Both the people of Italy and people in general will, if they detect they have no master over them, turn to rebellion and mutiny.

From Napoleon's letter of 8 March 1806

L Murat tries to rally Italians in support of the fugitive Napoleon who now renounced the Grand Empire

Rimini, March 30 1815 Providence is at last calling you to be an independent nation. From the Alps to the Straits of Sicily can be heard a single cry: 'Italian independence!' By what title do foreigners deny you this primary right of every people? By what right do they lord it over your beautiful country, taking your wealth elsewhere, conscripting your children to fight and die far from the tombs of their ancestors? Was it in vain that nature created the Alps as your defence and gave you that even greater barrier provided by differences of language, customs and character? No! Away with foreign domination! You were once masters of the world, and have expiated your glory in twenty centuries of slaughter and oppression. But today you can recover that glory by breaking free from your masters [by whom he presumably now means the Austrians].

From *Proclamation to the Italians* by Marshal Murat

M The poem written by Manzoni on Napoleon's death in 1821 is quoted in the Italian language which Manzoni prized

Dall'Alpi alle Piramidi,
Dal Manzanarre al Reno,
Di quel securo il fumine
Tenea dietro al baleno;
Scoppiò da Scilla al Tanai,
Dall'uno all'altro mar.

Ei si nomò: due secoli,
L'un contro l'altro armato,
Sommessi a lui si volsero,

Come aspettando il fato;
Ei fe'silenzio, ed arbitro
S'assise in mezzo a lor.

From the Alps to the Pyramids,
From Madrid to the Rhine,
That man, who was so sure of himself,
Made the thunderbolt directly follow the lightning.
It exploded from Scilla [toe of Italy] to the Don [Russian river],
From one sea to the other.

He spoke his own name. Two centuries,
Armed one against the other,
Meekly turned towards him
As if awaiting their destiny.
He said nothing,
But sat between them as arbiter.

From *Il Cinque Maggio* [*The Fifth of May*] by A. Manzoni (1821), translated by Carolyn Cooksey

N Giuseppe Valeriani (1765–1856), who had participated in the Cisalpine Republic before becoming disillusioned, looks back on the Napoleonic years

There is no victory or revolution without great injustice. Revolution implies robbing the rich to give to the poor. ... In Italy, as in France, the princes and their followers were despoiled. Ecclesiastical property, and that of the religious communities, congregations, hospitals, communes and so on, was expropriated. Once the French – the cause of our internal discords – had enriched themselves and satisfied the greed of those Italians who had aided them, it was in the interest of the plunderers to put an end to anarchy. ... It was obvious that the established institutions, with their democratic names, in fact gave power to one man, and that the Cisalpine republicans were falling under a new yoke, in spite of the pompous protests of complete freedom, which the apostles repeated continually.

From *History of the Administration of the Italy under French Rule* by G. Valeriani (1823)

O But Giuseppe Pecchio (1785–1835), a liberal who had also taken part, lists the benefits of French rule

The numerous civil and military posts, the appointment of a body of engineers for public works, of over a thousand land-surveyors engaged in the new census, and lastly a law of inheritance ensuring a fairer distribution of property had increased the size, education and influence of the third estate (or the middle class), which is the basis of constitutional liberty. ... Under their old governments the provinces of the Kingdom of Italy became unaccustomed to the use of arms and so lost the feeling of glory. ... War and conscription miraculously convinced Italians that the enemies of their independence were no more valiant than they. Within a few years conscription had created an army of 80,000 soldiers in the Kingdom of Italy. Trained by the example of French valour, they ended by rivalling it.

From *Essay on the Financial Administration of the Kingdom of Italy from 1802 to 1814* by G. Pecchio (1830)

P Historian, Geoffrey Ellis, points to the specific benefits enjoyed by some Piedmontese families

Over the whole period from 1798 to 1810 the sales of *biens nationaux* [confiscated ecclesiastical land] in the 27th military division (which included Piedmont) exceeded 66 million francs, equivalent to roughly twice the average annual value of Piedmontese exports during those same years. They were dominated by a mixed group of old landowners, merchants, bankers and high office-holders. ... By comparison, the peasantry gained little. ... Among the noble families which came out well from the sales of the *biens nationaux* were the likes of Cavour, Balbo and d'Azeglio, all prominent later in the Risorgimento.

From *The Napoleonic Empire* by G. Ellis (1991)

Q Massimo d'Azeglio himself gives a rather different account of the effect of the French wars on his family

We had been very well off, but now we were in straits. ... All this rumpus had cost my father altogether 400,000 francs in hard cash; without reckoning the impoverishment of his land due to the incredible lack of labour; or the value of silver, jewels, etc, donated at the outbreak of war, similar offerings having been made by the Court and all the nobility. ...

I have been through a period of reaction; I know what that means; but not even that experience can ever make me regret the passing of Napoleon and French rule in Italy, although it is true that we were losing a government which ... was to lead to the triumph of principles which are the very life of human society; to go back once more to an inept government of bemused, prejudiced ignoramuses. Nobody considered this at the time, and even if they had done so, I think that all of us – certainly my father and I – would have said: 'Let the Devil himself come, but out with the French.'

From *Things I Remember* by M. d'Azeglio (1863)

The Making of Modern Italy

Questions

1. How useful are sources A–D and K in assessing French attitudes to the Italian people? **(7 marks)**
2. What benefits and what penalties of French rule are suggested in sources E–G? **(8 marks)**
3. How reliable are H–J as sources for the Italian counter-revolutionary movement? **(5 marks)**
4. Analyse the attitude towards Napoleon shown in source M. **(3 marks)**
5. Use sources L and N–Q to explore the links between the Napoleonic conquest of Italy and the development of Italian nationalism. **(7 marks)**

3 METTERNICH AND THE REPRESSION OF ITALY: 1815–31

'Italian affairs do not exist', announced the Austrian Chancellor, Prince Metternich, in 1814. His adviser, Gentz, put it another way: the states of Italy, 'squeezed between Austria and France', were 'deprived of any will of their own'. Representatives of the other Great Powers (Britain, Russia and Prussia), who gathered at Vienna to rearrange Europe after the defeat of Napoleon, also acted on this assumption. They used the Italian peninsula to further their general aims: to create a barrier of strong states around France, to restore 'legitimate' regimes and to preserve the balance of power. [A]

Thus the Treaty of Vienna strengthened France's south-eastern neighbour, Piedmont, by restoring its provinces of Savoy and Nice and giving it the Republic of Genoa. Where republics were concerned the Great Powers happily abandoned the principle of legitimacy. The old Venetian Republic also disappeared, becoming part of an enlarged Austrian region, Lombardy-Venetia. This manoeuvre formed part of a further strategy – that Austria should be a counter-weight against Russia. To that end, too, the states of central Italy were handed back to their previous Habsburg dukes or given new rulers from the Austrian royal house. An Austrian garrison was placed in the Papal States, where the Pope regained power. After the defeat of Murat in 1815 the Bourbon King Ferdinand I returned to the Two Sicilies, having signed a secret treaty with Austria that he would not grant a constitution. The whole peninsula was thus under Austrian control – a situation which Metternich was determined to preserve. [B]

It is hard to say how the Italian people would have responded to these arrangements had they been consulted. Many came out in the streets to welcome back the old dynasties. But secret sects like the *Carbonari*, which had been formed in the struggle against Napoleon, often turned against the Restoration settlement when vague Allied promises of constitutional liberty went unfulfilled. [C]

This happened in Piedmont. D'Azeglio describes King Victor Emmanuel I and his entourage returning to Turin (after an exile on the semi-feudal island of Sardinia) 'with powdered hair in pigtails and eighteenth-century tricorn hats ... amid the hurrahs of the crowd'. The King restored the *ancien régime*: he brought back internal customs, reinstated all religious orders, confined Jews to ghettoes and censored all writing. He further alienated his subjects by trying to stop them from using the roads built by the French. [D]

In Lombardy and Venetia the Habsburgs aimed to forestall opposition by ruling justly. But through heavy tariffs and conscription they soon provoked resentment, which they attempted to quell via spying and censorship. Unable to express their ideas legitimately, liberals increasingly joined secret organisations. [E]

The Habsburgs in central Italy ruled with varying degrees of success. Ferdinand III, Grand Duke of Tuscany, followed his predecessors by governing in a benevolent fashion. Even so, the Viennese authorities were apt to intervene – in 1833, for example, they suppressed the liberal journal *Antologia*, which had published some of the best new Italian writing. The Duchess of Parma, Napoleon's second wife Marie-Louise, ruled moderately. The same could not be said of Modena's new duke, Francis IV, who was so reactionary that he suspected anyone with a beard or moustache of sedition. [F]

The restored Pope Pius VII won widespread sympathy because of his years of cruel imprisonment by the French. In its spiritual role the papacy continued to command respect in Italy. But opposition to its worldly power grew after the Restoration, a time of severe economic hardship and (under Leo XII, who succeeded Pius in 1823) grim political repression. [G]

King Ferdinand of the Two Sicilies also aroused mixed feelings among his subjects. His Chief Minister, Luigi de Medici, retained the best of the Napoleonic reforms and extended them to Sicily (which the French had never conquered). Liberals became disaffected, however, once they realised there would be no representative government. The Sicilians too were resentful: they hankered after constitutional rule, having had a brief spell of it thanks to their British governor in 1812. All over the Kingdom deep-seated local rivalries festered and social tensions mounted in the harsh economic conditions of the post-war years. [H–I]

Naples belied Metternich's prediction that 'no Italians have the energy to revolt during the six long months of summer'. In July 1820 a group of young Neapolitan army officers and *Carbonari* organised a rebellion. Unable to rely on his troops, the King granted a constitution and appointed his son Regent – all without bloodshed. Inspired by news of this success, an improbable alliance of nobles and guild craftsmen in Palermo proclaimed a separate constitution for Sicily. In both cities the revolutionaries soon split into moderate and radical factions, and in Sicily there was virtual civil war since some areas of the island wanted to remain part of the kingdom. No one can say what type of government would have emerged from this confusion and how much popular support it would have commanded, since the King quickly appealed to the Austrians for military help.

Metternich and the Repression of Italy: 1815–31

The Great Powers, gathered in Congress at Troppau, considered the matter. Metternich, Tsar Alexander I and King Frederick William III of Prussia signed the Troppau Protocol, claiming for themselves 'the undisputed right' to 'eradicate all the evils which threatened to break out over Europe'. On 7 March 1821 Austrian troops crushed the Neapolitan rebels. [J]

By this time, however, their example had inspired discontented groups in Piedmont to plot against their reactionary monarch. Led by army officers, they proclaimed a radical constitution on 9 March and raised the tricolour flag in the name of a new 'Kingdom of Italy'. Victor Emmanuel abdicated in favour of his brother, Charles Felix, but appointed as Regent his young cousin, Charles Albert, who had, for reasons which remain obscure, encouraged the rebels. During the next few weeks moderates and democrats struggled for control, Charles Albert equivocated and the people of Piedmont took little interest in the proceedings. In April the Austrian army easily defeated the rebels. [K]

Hopelessly unsuccessful though these risings were, they frightened Italy's rulers into strong reprisals and greater dependence on Austria. Even in areas like Lombardy and the Papal States where there had been no revolution, mass political trials were held and liberals received heavy sentences. Writers such as Silvio Pellico spent many years in prison; others escaped abroad. Some of those fleeing from Piedmont passed through Genoa, where their plight so affected the 16-year-old Guiseppe Mazzini that he began to dress in black. He dedicated his life to their cause. [L–O]

Another flurry of liberal success followed the French Revolution of 1830, which overthrew the restored Bourbon dynasty and caused a tearful Metternich to announce that his life's work was destroyed. Exiles had for some years been plotting a revolution in central Italy, choosing as its unlikely figurehead the Duke of Modena. But before the rising began, in February 1831, the Duke betrayed the conspirators and arrested their leader in Italy, Ciro Menotti. Even so the rebels forced the Duke to flee and they also helped to bring down the government of Parma and the Papal administrations in Bologna and Reggio.

Once in power, though, the liberals could neither agree on a form of government nor arouse popular support. They had hoped for help from the new French republic but its Foreign Minister declared that 'the blood of Frenchmen belongs to France alone'. So there was little resistance in March when Austrian troops occupied all the affected cities and restored their legitimate rulers – apparently to the joy of the peasants. In May the Great Powers met in Rome to discuss how such troubles could be prevented in future. They suggested various reforms in a Memorandum to the new Pope (Gregory XVI) but he seems to have taken little notice of it. [P–Q]

The Making of Modern Italy

Menotti had by this time been executed; but, as Mazzini wrote, 'One cannot execute ideas, [which] ripen quickly when they are nourished by the blood of martyrs'. [R] Mazzini himself was arrested in 1830. During his short spell in prison he decided that Italy could not be freed by secret sects but only by the will of the whole people. With this aim in view he went to Marseilles after his release in February 1831 and founded the nationalist movement known as Young Italy. Metternich regarded him as 'the most dangerous man in Europe'.

A Metternich explains in 1814 that Italy is to be
... a combination of independent states, linked together by the same geographical expression. The Emperor has no ambitious designs on the peninsula but wishes only to extinguish the spirit of Italian unity and ideas about constitutions. ... Therefore he has refrained from calling himself 'King of Italy', and decided to dissolve the Italian army, and to abolish all Italian institutions which pointed towards the project or the existence of a great kingdom. ... Austria regards King Victor Emmanuel as the vanguard for the defence of the peninsula, for the maintenance of a durable peace, and for the overthrow of the spirit of Italian jacobinism.

From a conversation with the Piedmontese representative in Vienna

B The 1815 treaty between Austria and King Ferdinand promises
... to preserve their respective states and subjects from new reactions, and from the danger of imprudent innovations which would lead to such reactions.
... to allow no change which could not be reconciled with the ancient monarchical institutions, or with the principles adopted by His Imperial Majesty for the internal government of his Italian provinces.
... not to conclude any alliance contrary to the defensive federation of Italy.

From the secret treaty signed on 12 June 1815

C Metternich describes his first experience of Italy, which he found to be a 'fine' country with a 'divine' climate
My presence in Italy has an incalculable influence on the progress of affairs. ... The sovereign of all Italy could not be received as I am; all those who are on the right side – and they are very numerous – crowd round me; they have given me their entire confidence, and look for safety from me alone. The Jacobins hide themselves, and they look upon me as a rod held over them.

Letter from Metternich to his wife, 14 July 1817

D   The Piedmontese writer and artist, d'Azeglio, was surprised that
... the leaders and gentry, representing the restored governments, were so foolish as not to understand how different people were in 1814 from what they had been in 1789. They could not persuade themselves that under no circumstances would men renounce those benefits created by the genius of Napoleon and the march of time, to which they had grown accustomed. Rulers and ministers, back from exile, found it convenient to accept Napoleon's legacy, disclaiming liability. They kept police, bureaucracy, taxes, disproportionately large armies, etc; but the good legal and administrative system, the stimulation given to merit and the sciences, class equality, the improvement and extension of communications, liberty of conscience, and so many other excellent features of the rule of the great warrior they threw out of the window. In Italy ... the new despotism, could be defined as: Napoleon dressed as a Jesuit!

From *Things I Remember* by M. d'Azeglio (1863)

E   The Austrian police in Venice are told their secret duties
Seeking out and unmasking conspiracies, plots, plans, undertakings and enterprises which tend to endanger the safety of the sacred person of His Majesty ... and all influences that might be detrimental to the internal and external public safety of the monarchy.
Watching and directing public feeling in all classes of inhabitants, and their views on political events; surveillance over anyone who exercises a major influence on public feeling and over anyone who invents or propagates false, faked, or alarming news; keeping a watch on remarks, judgements, complaints or desires made about public dispositions and measures, such as those regarding the administration of the state ...
Keeping a watch over the influence on public opinion *of gazettes, newspapers, pamphlets, books or pictures* of any sort, but especially *if they are of a political nature* ...

From the secret files of the Austrian police, c. 1820

F   One of the first journals to encourage Italian revival was *Il Conciliatore* [*The Conciliator*], published in Milan from September 1818 to October 1819, when it was closed down by the Austrian Government
Italy, and Lombardy in particular, is an agricultural and trading country. Land is much divided among its citizens and wealth flows uniformly, so to speak, through all the arteries of the state. Realizing this, *Il Conciliatore* knows that it must discuss good farming methods, the invention of new machines, the division of labour, in short, the art

The Making of Modern Italy

of multiplying wealth: an art which benefits the state but which is largely left, by its very nature, to the wits and activities of individuals. ... Sometimes we shall have to describe the customs of this or that country, of this or that social class. ... Sometimes, finally, we shall have to concern ourselves with those principles of legislation, which, infiltrated in various guises into the institutions of ancient and modern peoples, help to mould their character and fix their customs. ... However, the seriousness of these subjects would make our Journal too dull if we did not propose always to include some entertaining studies of literature.

From *Il Conciliatore*, 3 September 1818

G   A liberal Italian historian (who was involved in the politics of his day) describes the measures introduced by the second Restoration Pope, Leo XII

Being resolved to change the policy of the state, and bring it back, as far as possible, to the ancient rules and customs, which he thought admirable, he set about carrying these plans into effect with a persevering anxiety. ... He gave countenance and protection to every kind of religious congregation and pious confraternity; ... he appointed that education should be brought entirely under the ecclesiastical hierarchy; he determined to have all institutions of charity and beneficence administered and governed by the clergy; he confirmed and enlarged the clerical exemptions, privileges and jurisdictions. He took away from the Jews the right to hold real property ... [and] caused them to be shut up in Ghettoes with walls and gates. ... The result was that many wealthy and honourable merchants emigrated to Lombardy, to Venice, to Trieste, and to Tuscany. He dissolved the board which superintended vaccination, and quashed its rules; ... he reduced the municipalities to dependence on the government, made stringent game and fishery laws, enjoined the use, or to speak more truly, the torture, of the Latin language in forensic speaking and writing and in the universities.

From *The Roman State from 1815 to 1850* by L. C. Farini (1853), translated by W. E. Gladstone, the English statesman

H   Members of the *Carbonari* are instructed in their aims

Aims of the Order. The independence of Italy, our Country. To give her a single, constitutional government ... based on a constitution, freedom of the press and of worship, the same laws, currency and measures.

Methods of the Order. To spread liberal ideas and communicate them to adherents, friends and clerics, by firmly convincing them of the unfortunate state of affairs of our Mother Country. The press, gatherings and private conversations are opportune means. Cunning and perseverance are needed and, above all, the eradication of all kinds of prejudice. The unprejudiced peasant is more enthusiastic than the rich man, the property owner, and is therefore more useful.

I   But the *Sanfedisti*, one of the popular Catholic sects devoted to wiping out liberalism, use a different oath
I swear to remain steadfast in the defence of the holy cause which I have embraced, not to spare anyone belonging to the infamous gang of liberals, regardless of his birth, lineage or fortune; to show no pity for the wailing of children or the old; and to spill the blood of the infamous liberals to the last drop, regardless of sex or rank. Finally I swear implacable hatred against all enemies of our Holy Roman Catholic religion, the only true one.

J   Metternich's letters record his reactions to Italian events
19 July 1820 The Neapolitan event is beyond all calculation; the consequences will be quickly seen, the remedies must not be waited for. ... Here is the first liberal movement: two squadrons of cavalry overturn a throne, and throw all the world into inexpressible troubles. ... Blood will flow in streams. A semi-barbarous people, of absolute ignorance and boundless credulity, hot-blooded as the Africans, a people who can neither read nor write, whose last word is the dagger – such a people offers fine material for constitutional privileges!
31 December 1820 Our fire-engines were not full in July, otherwise we should have set to work immediately. ... The Demagogues and the Liberals, who at Naples call themselves *Carbonari* and *Muratistes*, are divided.
3 March 1821 The chorus of Liberals will now strike up in a beautiful manner. I enjoy it beforehand: that is, abuse from people whom I purposely tread under foot pleases me.
22 March 1821 If I calculate correctly we shall enter Naples tomorrow: this revolution will be annihilated. ... Our army has not lost one drop of blood, and has gained much glory, for no excess, not the slightest disorder, has taken place. They did not fire, because their fire could not be returned. Scouts were never employed, for the people everywhere came to meet our troops, received them as deliverers, and gave up to them the food they had concealed from the inquiries of their oppressors. ... If the peasants are asked where the hostile army actually is, they reply, 'They have fled: they have gone to eat *maccaroni*'.
31 March 1821 We shall finish the Piedmontese affair as we did the Neapolitan.

The Making of Modern Italy

K   D'Azeglio gives his verdict on the Piedmontese revolution in which he did not become involved

However much I esteem some of the leaders of that revolution and however much friendship I feel for them, I must say quite frankly that I cannot approve of it or the methods by which it was brought about. A people cannot be moved except by something it knows or, at least, wants. Therefore, before starting to act, you must explain what you are doing, or, at least, rouse passions and desires. ... In Italy in 1821, the memories of military insolence, of the continental blockade, of the violent annexations and divisions of provinces and kingdoms ... had not been cancelled by five or six years of the restored monarchy. In the opinion of the majority, by the law of nature always the least intelligent, the restoration was a return to life, to tranquillity, to happiness; a liberation from a hated tyranny. ... The mass was therefore very far from wanting change. ... It all came down to an isolated effervescence, starting in the bosom of the secret societies, which did not, could not, spread to the rest of the nation, because their ideas were not properly understood and the changes they proclaimed were not wanted.

From *Things I Remember* by M. d'Azeglio (1863)

L   Mazzini describes his encounter with the Piedmontese rebels

One Sunday in April 1821, while I was yet a boy, I was walking in the Strada Nuova of Genoa with my mother and an old friend of our family. The Piedmontese insurrection had just been crushed; partly by Austria, partly through treachery, and partly through the weakness of its leaders.

  The revolutionists, seeking safety by sea, had flocked to Genoa, and, finding themselves distressed for means, they went about seeking help to enable them to cross into Spain where the revolution was yet triumphant. ... We were stopped and addressed by a tall black-bearded man with a severe and energetic countenance and a fiery glance that I have never forgotten. He held out a white handkerchief towards us, merely saying, *For the refugees of Italy*. My mother and friend dropped some money into the handkerchief, and he turned from us to put the same request to others. ... The remembrance of those refugees, many of whom became my friends in after life, pursued me wherever I went by day, and mingled with my dreams by night. I would have given I know not what to follow them. I began collecting names and facts, and studied as best I might the records of that heroic struggle, seeking to fathom the causes of its failure.

From *Life and Writings of Mazzini* (1864)

Metternich and the Repression of Italy: 1815–31

M Among the contributors to *Il Conciliatore* was Silvio Pellico, who was also a member the *Carbonari* in Milan. For these activities he spent ten years in prison

Near the walls of the city of Brunn, rises a hillock bestridden by the ill-fated fortress of the Spielberg, once the palace of the lords of Moravia, now the harshest prison of the Austrian Monarchy. ... There some 300 convicts, most of them robbers and murderers, were serving sentences, some of 'hard', others of 'very hard' labour. 'Hard' labour means to do forced labour, be chained by the ankle, sleep on bare boards, and eat the poorest imaginable food. ... As political prisoners we had been condemned to hard labour. ... After being handed over to the Superintendent, Maroncelli and I were led down into an underground passage where the doors of two very dark cells, not adjacent, were opened for us. There we were shut up, each in his den. ... Our prison garb consisted of a pair of trousers of rough cloth, the right leg grey, the left a Capuchin brown; a smock of the same two colours ... and a jacket similarly coloured. The stockings were made of coarse wool, the shirt of rough hemp full of prickles, a real hairshirt. ... Fetters on our feet, consisting of a chain from one leg to the other, gave a finishing touch to this outfit.

From *My Prisons* by Silvio Pellico (1832)

N A picture of Pellico's cell in the Spielberg, a reconstruction of which can be seen in the Museum of the Risorgimento in Turin

The Making of Modern Italy

O   The English poet, Lord Byron, who lived in Italy, expresses his sympathy with the nationalist movement

February 18 1821 It is no great matter, supposing that Italy could be liberated, who or what is sacrificed. It is a grand object – the very *poetry* of politics. Only think – a free Italy!!!

June 23 1821 You have no idea what a state of oppression this country is in – they arrested above a thousand of high and low throughout Romagna – banished some and confined others, without *trial, process*, or even *accusation*!! Everybody says they would have done the same by me if they dared proceed openly.

May 29 1823 So many changes have taken place since that period in the Milan circle that I hardly dare recur to it; – some dead, some banished, and some in the Austrian dungeons. – Poor Pellico! I
trust that, in his iron solitude, his Muse is consoling him in part – one day to delight us again, when she and her Poet are restored to freedom.

From letters by Lord Byron

P   Claiming to express 'the manifest wishes of the people' and 'the general will', the rebels of Bologna declare their independence from the Pope

Article 1: The temporal power of the Roman Pontiff over this city and province is legally at an end for ever.
Article 2: A general assembly of the people is summoned to choose deputies who will form a new government.
Article 3: This will soon be explained in more detail when other nearby cities have joined us and we know how many deputies are to be elected. A legal national representation will then come into existence.

From the Proclamation by the Provisional Government of Bologna, 8 February 1831

Q   In vain, the Great Powers recommend 'timely ameliorations' in the government of the Papal States

1. The improvements should take effect, not only in those provinces where the revolution burst out [in 1831], but also in those which remained faithful, and in the capital [Rome].
2. The laity [non-clergy] should be generally admitted to administrative and judicial functions. ...

The general re-establishment and appointment of municipalities elected by the people; and the institution of municipal privileges,

Metternich and the Repression of Italy: 1815-31

which shall govern the action of the bodies corporate, according to the local interests of the communities.

From a Memorandum to Pope Gregory XVI by Austria, Britain, France, Prussia and Russia, 21 May 1831

R A Modenese print honours the martyrdom of Ciro Menotti

The Making of Modern Italy

Questions

1 Explain the meaning of the following phrases as they are used in the sources:
   (a) 'geographical expression' (source A, line 2) **(2 marks)**
   (b) 'Italian jacobinism' (source A, line 10) **(2 marks)**
   (c) 'principles adopted by His Imperial Majesty for the internal government of his Italian provinces' (source B, lines 5–6) **(2 marks)**
2 What reliable information do sources D, E, G and Q give about the nature of Restoration governments in Italy? **(6 marks)**
3 How useful are sources C, F, H and I for finding out about the attitudes of Italian people in this period? **(6 marks)**
4 Assess the value of sources J–L and P in explaining the failure of Italian revolution in 1820–21 and 1831. **(6 marks)**
5 Which of sources L–O and R most vividly conveys the effects of repressive government during this period? **(6 marks)**

4 MAZZINI AND DREAMS OF A UNITED ITALY: 1831–47

'A more beautiful person I never beheld': Thomas Carlyle's view of Mazzini's character and appearance made a striking contrast to that of Metternich. The two men met in England in 1837 after Mazzini was expelled from Switzerland, where he had been hunted by Austrian agents. He was to spend nearly all the rest of his life as a poor exile in London, where he attracted the friendship and support of other writers, including Dickens and George Eliot, as well as the hero-worship of English working-class people, many of whom had pictures of him in their homes.

Mazzini devoted his time and energy to writing letters (50 000 in all), journals and pamphlets, to promote the cause of Young Italy. He dreamt of a revolution which would unite Italy as a single state with a democratic, republican government. Despite the efforts of Austrian, Italian and occasionally even English censors, some of this propaganda went into circulation. Many educated Italians were influenced not only by Mazzini's ideas but also by his example. A few were so inspired that they took part in ill-fated plots like that of the Bandiera brothers: in 1844, with 19 followers and against Mazzini's advice, they tried to start a revolution in Calabria but were soon betrayed, and shot by the Neapolitan authorities. Such failures demonstrate that the Italian masses, whom Mazzini loved, were hardly aroused by his efforts. After all, as he himself lamented, 'the people cannot read'. [A–D]

Mazzini was not the only patriotic writer trying to appeal to the Italian reading public during the 1840s. His main competitors were moderates who disagreed with his radical views. In his account of his long imprisonment in Austria, for example, Silvio Pellico denounced revolutionary activities and bore 'witness to the excellent Catholic religion' which had consoled him behind bars. Thus in 1832 *My Prisons* got past the censors and it was frequently reissued. For all its mild tone the book did much to arouse anti-Austrian feeling in Italy and, belatedly, Metternich tried to persuade the Pope to put it on the Index [the list of books forbidden to Catholic readers].

Another writer who was careful to avoid overt criticism of Austria was the Piedmontese priest, Vincenzo Gioberti. His *Moral and Civil Primacy of the Italians* (usually referred to simply as the *Primato*) condemned Mazzini's concept of a unitary democratic republic and advocated a federation of Italian states under the leadership of the Pope, with no mention of constitutional reform. Five thousand copies of this long-winded but persuasive book were printed in 1843 and it continued to be read by many pious middle-class Italians. [E]

Fellow Piedmontese moderates like d'Azeglio and his cousin, Cesare Balbo, agreed with much of the *Primato* but found the idea of Papal leadership both unappealing and impractical; Gioberti had not explained how the notoriously conservative papacy was to be persuaded to undertake its new role. In 1844 Balbo published *The Hopes of Italy*, suggesting that Austria could be bribed with Balkan territory to give up its Italian possessions and that Italian rulers should come together in a confederation led by Piedmont. In his pamphlet, *Recent Events in the Romagna* (1846), d'Azeglio condemned an attempted revolution in the Papal States and encouraged the Pope's subjects to look to Piedmont for help in ridding themselves of despotic rule. Moderate though they were, the works of Gioberti, Balbo and d'Azeglio could not be published in Piedmont, where King Charles Albert had forsworn any youthful liberal leanings since his accession in 1824 and now forbade the use of such words as 'nation', 'liberty' and 'Italy'. Nevertheless the 'dangerous' literature did circulate and it helped to make the idea of unification respectable. [F–G]

Creative writers of the Romantic movement also contributed to the growth of Italian consciousness. The exiled poet Ugo Foscolo was a strong influence on Mazzini (who knew his poem *Tombs* by heart) and on Garibaldi (who had a book of Foscolo's poems open at his bedside when he died). The greatest nineteenth-century Italian poet, Giacomo Leopardi, also used patriotic themes. Poetry was only read by a small minority but Alessandro Manzoni's famous novel, *The Betrothed*, quickly became a bestseller after its publication in Milan (1825–7). The story of a peasant betrothal threatened by aristocratic plots, riots, injustice, invasion and plague is set in seventeenth-century Lombardy (then ruled by Spain) and has no obvious connection with the Risorgimento. Its identification with the Italian cause is due less to its subject matter than to the fact that in 1842 Manzoni rewrote it in Tuscan (rather than the Milanese dialect he had originally used), thus helping to ensure that the language of Dante became that of Italy. [H–K]

Another nationalist member of Milan's cultural elite was the composer Giuseppe Verdi, a close friend of Manzoni. During the 1840s, when writing his earlier operas, Verdi looked for themes which would nourish growing patriotism without breaking Austrian laws against disrespect for sovereigns and praise for Italian independence. His solution was to use stories from other countries (as in *Nabucco* and *Macbeth*) or from Italian history (as in *The Battle of Legnano*). Since it was not necessary to be rich to buy tickets for the pit, to be literate to appreciate the meaning of choruses, or to be restrained in responding to the music, performances of Verdi's operas often resembled nationalist demonstrations – or even modern football matches. When the outraged Venetian authorities stopped audiences at *Macbeth* from throwing red and green bouquets onto the stage they hurled flowers of yellow and black (the Austrian colours) on which the singers then trampled. The singing of the *Macbeth* chorus, 'The Fatherland Betrayed', at La Scala may well have helped to provoke the Milanese revolution of 1848. [L]

The idea of unification was also spread in more prosaic ways during the 1840s. Regular scientific congresses were held in different Italian cities – at the first one, which took place at Pisa in 1839, the opening speaker urged delegates to 'increase the glory of the Italian nation'. Carlo Cattaneo's influential journal *Il Politecnico* published articles on such practical matters as the abolition of customs duties between states. Even railway enthusiasts played their part: the wealthy journalist Count Camillo Cavour argued that a planned rail system would be of great benefit to Italy as a whole. His view must have upset Pope Gregory XVI who prohibited the building of railways in the Papal States on the grounds that they might bring 'malcontents' to Rome and 'work harm to religion'. [M–P]

In 1846, however, this reactionary Pontiff died and his successor, Pius IX (*Pio Nono*), immediately demonstrated a comparative liberalism by releasing over a thousand political prisoners. At about the same time King Charles Albert of Piedmont became impatient with Austrian domination (not least because of the prohibitive duties on Piedmontese wine) and tentatively suggested that Italians should hope for liberation. In 1847 he freed the press from censorship, enabling Cavour and Balbo to found a newspaper entitled *Il Risorgimento*. Meanwhile the new British Foreign Minister, Lord Palmerston, expressed cautious sympathy for Italian nationalism and sent Lord Minto on a special mission to Turin, Florence and Rome. In 1847 Metternich reiterated his famous dictum that 'Italy is a geographical expression'; but Mazzini, watching events from England, felt sure that his dream of a united Italy was about to come true. [Q–S]

A   Mazzini spells out the aims of Young Italy in 1831

Young Italy is a brotherhood of Italians who believe in the law of progress and duty, and are convinced that Italy is destined to become one nation, convinced also that she possesses sufficient strength within herself to become one, and that the ill success of her former efforts is to be attributed not to weakness, but to the misdirection of revolutionary elements within her, and that the secret force lies in constancy and unity of effort. . . .

Young Italy is republican and unitarian – republican because theoretically every nation is destined, by the law of God and humanity, to form a free and equal community of brothers; and the republican form of government is the only one which ensures this future. ...

Young Italy is unitarian, because, without unity there is no true nation; because, without unity there is no real strength; and Italy, surrounded as she is by powerful and jealous nations, has need of strength above all things; ... because federalism, by reviving the local rivalries now extinct, would throw Italy back upon the Middle Ages; and because federalism, by destroying the unity of the great Italian family, would strike at the root of the great mission Italy is destined to accomplish for humanity. ...

The means by which Young Italy proposes to reach its aim are education and insurrection, to be adopted simultaneously and made to harmonise with each other. Education must ever be directed to teach, by example, word and pen, the necessity of insurrection. Insurrection, whenever it can be realised, must be so conducted as to render it a means of national education.

B It became known in 1844 that Mazzini's letters were being intercepted by the British Conservative Government. Lord Aberdeen, the Foreign Secretary, defends this practice

Representations had been made to the British Government from high sources, that plots of which M. Mazzini was the centre were carrying on, upon British territory, to excite an insurrection in Italy; and that such insurrection, should it form a formidable aspect, would, from peculiar political circumstances, disturb the peace of Europe. The British Government, considering the extent to which British interests were involved in the maintenance of that peace, issued ... a warrant to open and detain M. Mazzini's letters. Such information deduced from those letters as appeared to the British Government calculated to frustrate this attempt was communicated to a foreign power [Austria]; but the information so communicated was not of a nature to compromise ... the safety of any individual within the reach of that foreign power.

An extract from the report of a secret committee in *Westminster Review* (1844)

C   These revelations did much to increase popular sympathy for Mazzini, a special portrait of whom was printed in *The Pictorial Times* (7 September 1844)

JOSEPH MAZZINI.

D   Mazzini took the opportunity of this furore to write in English and to publish, at his own expense, a pamphlet criticising the British government and explaining Italian grievances

I am only astonished that in the midst of Parliament, where these words were uttered [in defence of the spying], no one rose amongst all those who have recently travelled to Italy, or who study her history ... to say to him: 'Security! peace! independence! my Lord! that is precisely what the man is seeking for his country whose correspondence your colleagues have violated – it is what was sought by those men who were shot some months since in Calabria [the Bandiera brothers], possibly in consequence of this violation. There is no *security* except under laws, under wise laws voted by the best men, sanctioned by the love of the people; and there are no laws in Italy: there is instead the caprice of eight detested masters, and of a handful of men chosen by these masters to second their caprice.' ...

We Italians have neither Parliament, nor hustings, nor liberty of the press, nor liberty of speech, nor possibility of lawful public assemblage, nor a single means of expressing the opinion stirring within us. Italy is a vast prison, guarded by a certain number of gaolers and gendarmes, supported in case of need by the bayonets of men whom we don't understand and who don't understand us. If we speak they thrust a gag on our mouths; if we make a show of action, they platoon us. A petition, signed *collectively*, constitutes a crime against the State. Nothing is left to us but the endeavour to agree in secret to wrench the bars from the doors and windows of our prison – to knock down gates and gaolers, that we may breathe the fresh life-giving air of liberty, the air of God.

From *Italy, Austria and the Pope* by Mazzini (1845)

E Gioberti puts forward his view of Italy's 'sublime vocation'

I propose to prove that Italy contains within herself, above all through religion, all the conditions required for her national and political resurrection or *risorgimento*, and that to bring this about she has no need of revolutions within and still less of foreign invasions or foreign exemplars. And to begin with I say that Italy must first and foremost regain her life as a nation; and that her life as a nation cannot come into being without some degree of union between her various members. ...

That the Pope is naturally, and should be effectively, the civil head of Italy is a truth forecast in the nature of things, confirmed by many centuries of history, recognised on past occasions by the peoples and princes of our land, and only thrown into doubt by those commentators who drank at foreign springs and diverted their poison to the motherland.

The benefits Italy would gain from a political confederation under the moderating authority of the pontiff are beyond enumeration. For such a cooperative association would increase the strength of the various princes without damaging their independence, and would put the strength of each at the disposal of all: it would remove the causes of disruptive wars and revolutions at home, and make foreign invasions impossible; inasmuch as Italy, dominated by the Alps and girt by the sea, can resist the onslaughts of half Europe only if we are united; it would give us anew an honour we had in bygone times by placing Italy in the first rank of Powers.

From *The Moral and Civil Primacy of the Italians* by V. Gioberti (1843)

F The Piedmontese politician and historian, Cesare Balbo, finds Mazzini's dream of a united Italy ludicrous

The unitary solution is childish, no more than the fantasy of rhetorical schoolboys, two-a-penny poets and café politicians. ... Confederations are the type of constitution most suited to Italy's nature and history.

... The only obstacle to an Italian confederation – a most serious obstacle – is foreign rule, which penetrates deep into the peninsula. ... An Italian confederation is neither desirable nor possible if a foreign power forms part of it. ... A democratic insurrection may continue for some time to be the fear of the police or the hope of secret societies, but it cannot be considered as part of any foreseeable future, it cannot be a possibility, or an event to be reckoned on as part of any major undertaking.

In the course of the eighteenth century the monarchy of Savoy [Piedmont] increased by a third in population and almost doubled in territory. Equally notable is the method by which these additions were acquired, all at the expense of Austria, for the most part by fighting for them. Should such an example be imitated in similar circumstances, or should it be avoided because the times have changed? One can only decide on each occasion.

From *The Hopes of Italy* by C. Balbo (1844)

G   D'Azeglio recommends continual pressure on public opinion, which will achieve Italy's aims 'with our hands in our pockets'

To protest against injustices, openly, publicly, in every way, on every possible occasion, is, in my opinion, the formula that best expresses the greatest necessity of our times, the most useful and the most potent action now. The first, the greatest protest, which we should never tire of making, which should sound on every tongue, flow from every pen, must be against foreign occupation, and in support of our right to full control over our own soil, of our nationality, and of our independence. Let protests follow against the injustices, the abuses and evil orders of our own governments.

From *Recent Events in the Romagna* by M. d'Azeglio (1845)

H   Leopardi's poem *All'Italia* [*To Italy*] expresses the romantic patriotism of his day

A patria mia, vedo le mura e gli archi
E le colonne e i simulacri e l'ermi
Torre degli avi nostri,
Ma la gloria non vedo ...

O my fatherland, I see the walls
And the arches and the columns and
the crumbling towers of our ancestors,
but the glory I do not see ...

From Leopardi's poem *All'Italia*, published in 1818

The Making of Modern Italy

I   Manzoni's peasant couple, united at last
... came to the conclusion that troubles often come to those who bring them on themselves, but that not even the most cautious and innocent behaviour can ward them off; and that when they come – whether by our own fault or not – confidence in God can lighten them and turn them to our own improvement. This conclusion, though it was reached by poor people, has seemed so just to us that we have thought of putting it down here, as the juice of the whole tale.

From *The Betrothed* by A. Manzoni (1827, rewritten 1842)

J   This religious tone upset anti-clerical patriots like Luigi Settembrini
To write and publish in 1827, in the darkest and most ferocious time of reaction, when the priests were in command, the Austrians were terrorizing Venetia and Lombardy, and tyrants were up in arms everywhere, a book which praised priests and friars and advised patience, submission, and pardon, meant (Manzoni certainly didn't want this, but it is the necessary consequence of the book) to advise submission to slavery, the negation of patriotism and of every generous sentiment.

From a lecture by Settembrini published (after his death) in 1909

K   But Mazzini defended Italian romantics like Manzoni as
... men for whom truth is the *aim*, and nature and the heart the *mean*.
... They are not slaves of foreign ideas; they want to give Italy an original national literature, a literature which is not just a sound of fugitive music, but one which soothes the ear and yet interprets the emotions, ideas, and needs of the social movement.

From an article by Mazzini in *L'Indicatore Genovese* (1828), a journal started and suppressed in that year

L   'The Chorus of the Hebrew Slaves' from Verdi's *Nabucco* (1841)
Va, pensiero, sull' ali dorate;
va, ti posa sui clivi, sui colli,
ove olezzano tepide e molli
l'aure dolci del suolo natal!
Del Giordano le rive saluta,
di Sionne le torri atterrate ...
Oh, mi patria sì bella e perduta!
Oh, membranza si cara e fatal!
Arpa d'ôr dei fatidici vati,
perchè muta dal salice pendi?

Le memorie nel petto raccendi,
ci favella del tempo che fu!
O simile di Solima ai fati
traggi un suono di crudo lamento,
O t'ispiri il Signori un concento
che ne infonda al patire virtù!

Go, my thought, on golden wings;
go, alight upon the slopes, the hills,
where, soft and warm, the sweet breezes
of our native land are fragrant!
Greet the banks of the Jordan
And Zion's razed towers ...
Oh, my country so lovely and lost!
Oh, remembrance so dear and ill-fated!
Golden harp of the prophetic bards,
why do you hang mute on the willow?
Rekindle the memories in our breasts,
speak to us of the times of yore!
Just as for the cruel fate of Jerusalem,
intone a strain of bitter lamentation,
Otherwise let the Lord inspire you with
a melody to give us strength to suffer!

M A professor at Pisa University believed that scientific congresses had beneficial effects in Tuscany

When urged to have scientific congresses as in other countries, Grand Duke Leopold allowed this, though they were prohibited from discussing the moral and political sciences. The first of these meetings was held at Pisa late in 1839, and another, with extraordinary pomp, at Florence in 1841. ... Flattered by the praises of the scientific world ... Leopold then aimed at drawing Italy's illustrious men of learning to Tuscany, regardless of their political opinions. [After a time] every city had a group of liberals who carefully read various illicit publications and maintained relationships with other groups elsewhere. ... By means of writings, discussions and gatherings they ingeniously inculcated ideas of liberalism into the minds of the common people. Of all the Tuscans, it was among the common people of Leghorn that the religion of the motherland counted its most ardent devotees; and in the Venezia quarter, a substantial number of ordinary workmen held meetings every Sunday to read some piece of the liberal gospel.

From *History of Tuscany* by G. Montanelli (1853)

N The Milanese scientific journalist, Carlo Cattaneo, was more sceptical about the unifying effects of intellectual debate

We are convinced that Italy above all must keep in unison with Europe, and not cherish any other national sentiment than that of retaining a worthy place in the scientific association of Europe and the world. Peoples should act as a permanent mirror to each other, because the interests of civilisation are mutually dependent and common; because science is one, art is one, glory is one. The nation of scholarly men is one ... it is the nation of intellectuals, which inhabits all climates and speaks all languages. Beneath this nation there is a multitude divided into a thousand discordant *patria* [homelands], castes, dialects, into greedy, bloodthirsty factions, which revel in superstition, egoism, ignorance, which sometimes even love and defend ignorance as if it were the principle of life and the basis of customs and society.

From an article by Cattaneo in *Il Politecnico* (1839)

Mazzini and Dreams of a United Italy: 1831–47

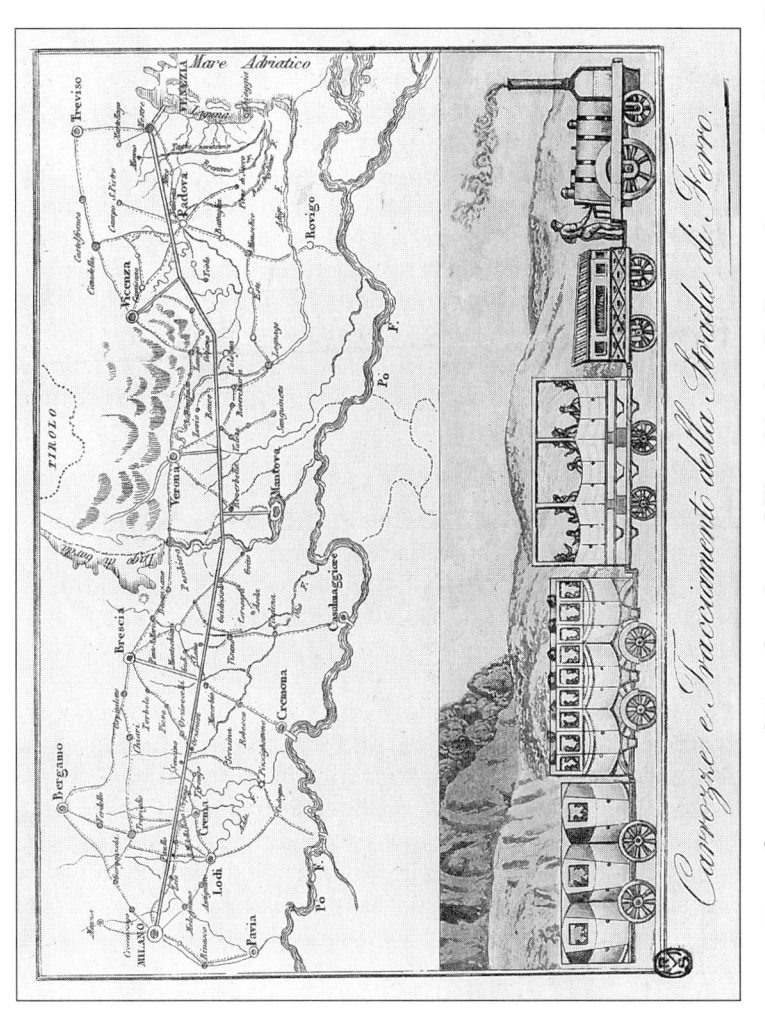

O Cattaneo was secretary of a committee planning a Milan–Venice Railway; he wanted it to link the cities (and therefore the citizens) of Lombardy and Venetia rather than take the shortest route favoured by the engineers, which is shown on this map. The Austrians wanted a line which would link up easily with Vienna. As a result of these disputes, as well as lack of capital, only small sections had been built by 1846

The Making of Modern Italy

P The idea of a national railway system was considered so subversive that a proposal for it by the Piedmontese Carlo Petitti had to be published in Paris, as did this review by another Piedmontese, Count Cavour

The lines which connect Genoa, Leghorn and Naples with Trieste, Venice, Ancona and the east coast of the Kingdom of Naples, will conduct a great wave of merchandise and travellers across Italy from the Mediterranean to the Adriatic. ... The railways will open a magnificent economic future for Italy and should provide her with the means to regain the brilliant commercial position that she held throughout the Middle Ages. Nevertheless, however great the material benefits to Italy from railways, they are much less important than the inevitable moral effects. The prime cause [of Italy's troubles] is the political influence which foreigners have exercised on us for centuries, and the principal obstacles opposed to throwing off this baleful influence are ... the internal divisions, the rivalries, the antipathy that different parts of our great Italian family hold for each other; ... if the action of the railways diminishes these obstacles and perhaps even abolishes them, it will give the greatest encouragement to the spirit of Italian nationality.

From an article by Cavour in *Revue Nouvelle* (May 1846)

Q After his return from the Papal States in 1845 d'Azeglio was granted an audience with King Charles Albert

I told him at length of the disgust of all honest, sensible men at the Mazzinian foolishness and wickedness; of the suggestion made that I should start to do something or other to try to give a new and better direction to the people's activities; and of the excellent disposition I had found, with a few exceptions, wherever I went. 'All are persuaded that without force nothing can be done; and that the only force in Italy is that of Piedmont. ... Perhaps your Majesty will tell me if he approves, or not, of what I have done and what I have now said.'

He said quietly but firmly, without any hesitation or turning his glance away, but looking me straight in the eyes: 'Let those gentlemen know that they should remain quiet and take no steps now, as nothing can be done at present; but they can rest assured that when the opportunity arises, *my life, my children's lives, my arms, my treasure, my army; all shall be given to the cause of Italy.*' Expecting something quite different, I remained for a moment speechless. The intentions he had so resolutely revealed to me had so surprised me that they did not yet seem real. ... An inner voice repeated that terrible phrase: 'Don't trust him.'

A posthumous addition, authenticated by his daughter, to *Things I Remember* by d'Azeglio (1863)

Mazzini and Dreams of a United Italy: 1831–47

R   Lord Minto is dispatched to Italy with instructions from Palmerston to give cautious support to the 'liberal inclinations of the new Pope'

Her Majesty's Government are deeply impressed with the conviction that it is wise for sovereigns and their governments to pursue, in the administration of their affairs, a system of progressive improvement. ... And Her Majesty's Government consider ... that if an independent sovereign ... shall think it fit to make within his dominions such improvements in the laws and institutions of his country as he may think conducive to the welfare of his people, no other Government can have the right to attempt to restrain or to interfere. ... Her Majesty's Government would not see with indifference any aggression committed upon the Roman territories, with a view to preventing the Papal Government from carrying into effect those internal improvements which it might think proper to adopt.

From a letter from Palmerston to Lord Minto, November 1847

S   Mazzini is encouraged by reports from Europe in 1847

The democratic tendency of our times, the upward movement of the popular classes who desire to have their share in political life (hitherto a privilege) is henceforth no utopian dream, no doubtful anticipation: it is a fact, a great European fact which occupies every mind, influences the proceedings of governments, defies all opposition.

From an article for the *People's Journal*, August 1846

Questions

1. To what extent do sources A–D reveal Mazzini as 'a dangerous conspirator'? **(5 marks)**
2. How appropriate is it to describe sources E–G as 'moderate'? **(5 marks)**
3. What do sources H–L suggest about the relevance of literature and opera to Italian nationalism? **(5 marks)**
4. Compare the assumptions made about Italian public opinion in sources M–P. **(5 marks)**
5. Which of sources Q–S offered the best grounds for hope to Italian nationalists in 1845–7? **(5 marks)**

5 CHARLES ALBERT AND *ITALIA FARÀ DA SÉ*: 1848–9

Two and a half years after making his surprising promises to d'Azeglio, King Charles Albert of Piedmont kept them by declaring war on Austria on 23 March 1848. He announced that, in standing up for her rights against the oppressor, Italy needed no assistance except that of God, whose 'helping hand' would enable her to do this on her own (*farà da sé*). What led this notoriously indecisive monarch to make such a rash claim and was it justified?

One reason for Charles Albert's trust in divine support was that God was already supposed to have 'given Pius IX to Italy'. Actually Charles Albert had been less enthusiastic than many other Italians about the Pope's liberal innovations. These included a free press and a National Guard (which even included women), as well as plans for education, poor relief and a railway system. In February 1848, under pressure, Pius went so far as to grant a constitution with a secular legislative body. Furthermore the Pope seemed to give his blessing to a united Italy. Even Mazzini thought that Pius might be able 'to unify Italy .. and achieve great, holy and enduring things'. Metternich predicted, more accurately, that 'if matters follow their natural course, he will be driven out of Rome'. [A]

Reforms in the Papal States encouraged other Italians to demand change from their own rulers. As early as November 1847 demonstrators in the Kingdom of Naples, shouting '*Viva Pio Nono*', called for political rights and (in Palermo) for Sicilian independence. In January 1848 armed crowds forced King Ferdinand to withdraw his troops from Sicily, which set up its own government. He also had to concede a constitution to the rest of his kingdom. [B]

These events were soon followed by the February revolution in France, which brought about the abdication of Louis Philippe and the creation of the Second Republic. All this alarmed Charles Albert, whose subjects also wanted more freedom. On 4 March he issued the *Statuto*, a constitution creating an elected assembly but reserving executive power for 'the King alone'. A new ministry was formed under the moderate nationalist, Cesare Balbo. The most urgent matter it had to decide was Piedmont's relationship with the neighbouring Austrian provinces, which were also in the throes of revolution. [C–E]

In both Lombardy and Venetia harsh economic circumstances sharpened Italians' discontent with Austrian rule. They particularly resented high taxation at a time of rising prices and unemployment, registering their feelings by refusing to smoke tobacco, on which there was a large Austrian duty. In Milan this protest led to riots. In Venice demonstrations were sparked off by the arrest of the popular lawyer, Daniele Manin, who had been voicing radical demands. The Paris revolution caused more excitement: Venetian gondoliers could 'talk of nothing but politics'. But in both regions it was the astonishing news of revolution in Vienna, leading to the fall of Metternich himself on 13 March, which precipitated full-scale insurrections. [F]

Their success was mainly due to the new weakness of the Austrian army. Already struggling to deal with uprisings in Vienna, Prague and Budapest, it now faced the desertion of many of its Italian soldiers in Milan and Venice. On 22 March the octogenarian Marshal Radetzky took 'the most frightful decision' of his life: he withdrew from Milan after five days of fighting. On the same day Daniele Manin declared an independent republic in Venice. His victory, like that of other leaders in 1848, stemmed from a remarkable revolutionary unity. The rival working-class gangs of Venice suspended their feuds. Peasants demonstrated solidarity with the anti-tobacco campaign by giving up their pipes. Manin appealed to his supporters by addressing them in simple dialect. But once the initial fervour had died down, tensions and divisions reappeared. [G–J]

One of the bitterest quarrels arose from Charles Albert's declaration of war on Austria. This was welcomed in Piedmont itself. Indeed, the King assumed that by leading his troops into battle and gaining territory he would become a popular hero. But his insistence that, in return for his help, the Lombards and Venetians must agree to 'fusion' with Piedmont caused much agonising. In Milan the republican Carlo Cattaneo refused to back the idea of union. To avoid too much dissension, however, he decided not to stand in the way of the moderates who were prepared to go along with it. Manin, also a strong republican, faced a similar dilemma. He was dismayed by the Austrian reconquest of much of Venetia and mistrustful of such supporters as the gondoliers, whose current song ran 'Fusion is really confusion'. So he urged the assembly on 4 July to vote for a provisional union with Piedmont. For a brief period (June–July 1848) a North Italian Kingdom came into existence. [L–M]

These political triumphs were not accompanied by sustained military success. Charles Albert was an incompetent general and refused to cooperate with Garibaldi's volunteer troops, who would bring 'dishonour to the army'. More seriously, after a Papal army had marched off to join the Piedmontese forces without his blessing, Pius IX issued an Allocution condemning the war and urging Italians not to fight. [K] Then, in May, King Ferdinand regained control of Naples

The Making of Modern Italy

and ordered his army to leave Lombardy. Many Papal and Neapolitan soldiers came home. Radetzky, on the other hand, rallied his forces and defeated Charles Albert at Custoza on 24 July. The King hastily signed an armistice, abandoning Milan to the Austrians and leaving Venice to fight on alone.

Manin did not think it essential for *Italia farà da sé*. He sought aid from the French Republic, which prepared an expeditionary force but decided not to send it. Manin also hoped for British help, but Palmerston's sympathy for Italian independence did not extend to intervention. For another year Venetians refused to surrender in spite of siege, starvation, bankruptcy and cholera. They carried on even when news came, in March 1849, that Austrian troops had repulsed a fresh attack by Charles Albert at Novara, causing the King to retreat and abdicate. When, on 13 August 1849, Manin decided that the city could no longer resist Austrian bombardment he hailed the Venetians, who had continued to support him despite his poor military leadership and his repressive rule. 'Such a people! To be forced to surrender with such a people!' [N]

Solidarity was lacking in the peninsula as a whole. Venice had received little financial help from the rest of Italy. Neapolitans were increasingly impatient with Sicilian separatism. In some areas peasants and the urban poor, finding that they gained nothing from revolutionary governments, turned back to the old regimes. Thus the *lazzari* of Naples helped royal troops to re-establish Bourbon power. And Lombard peasants shouted '*Viva Radetzky!*' as the Austrian army passed through their villages on its way back to Milan in July. On other occasions, though, radical groups won support as they sought to wage Mazzini's 'war of the people'. [O]

Their finest hour occurred in Rome. After the Allocution of April 1848 Pius IX lost most of his popularity. In November a general insurrection took place and he fled to Gaeta in the Kingdom of Naples. Early in 1849 the new government in Rome announced elections for an assembly to represent all Italy; this met in February and the Roman Republic was declared. When Mazzini arrived in Rome a month later he was immediately recognised as its natural leader. In practice the Republic did not represent Italy. Gioberti (now Prime Minister of Piedmont) accused Mazzini of being a greater enemy to Italy than the Austrians. The governments of Tuscany, Sicily and Venice, for various reasons of their own, rejected invitations to unite with it. The King of Naples, on the other hand, responded to the Pope's appeal for help and, along with Spain and Austria, dispatched troops to bring down the Republic. [P]

They were joined in April 1849 by Marshal Oudinot's expeditionary force, sent by the new French President, Louis Napoleon, who was anxious to win favour with his Catholic subjects. During his short period in power, Mazzini had ruled with modesty and tolerance; living in a single room and eating in a nearby *trattoria*, he passed measures of social justice which gained adherents among all classes. Because of this support, and thanks to the inspired military leadership of Garibaldi, Rome held out against its various enemies until the end of June. The republic then came to an end and the Pope was restored. Garibaldi left with his pregnant wife and 4000 followers to share 'long night watches, forced marches, and fighting at every step'. By August his army had dissolved and Anita Garibaldi had died. [Q–R]

Rome and Venice may have saved 'Italian honour', as Carlo Pisacane wrote, but all that remained of the year of revolutions was the constitution in Piedmont, now ruled by Charles Albert's son, Victor Emmanuel II. Mazzini returned to London and other revolutionaries went into exile. Italy had not succeeded in winning her own freedom. [S]

A Enthusiastic patriots interpreted this statement by the Pope as a call for unity

For Us especially – for Us as Head and Supreme Pontiff of the most holy Catholic religion – if We were unjustly assailed, is it possible that We should not find for our own defence innumerable sons who would support the centre of Catholic Unity as though it were their Father's house? A great gift from Heaven is this: one of the many gifts which He has bestowed on Italy; that a bare three million of our subjects possess two hundred million brothers of every nation and every tongue. In times very different from these, when the whole Roman world was disordered, this fact remained the salvation of Rome. Owing to it, the ruin of Italy was never complete. And this will always be her protection so long as the Apostolic See stands in her midst. Therefore, O Lord God, bless Italy and preserve for her this most precious gift of all – the faith!

From the Pope's *Motu Proprio*, 10 February 1848

B Luigi Settembrini, who had spent three years in a Neapolitan prison for republican activities, remembers the revolutions in Naples and Sicily

14 December 1847 A large crowd turned up and shouted: 'Long live Palermo and Sicily.' ... [Arrests were made] In the royal palace the King did nothing but discuss police matters. ... He frequently cursed Pius IX who had disturbed the hornet's nest, and expressed contempt for the weakness of Leopold of Tuscany and Charles Albert [both of whom had passed some reforms]; mounting his high horse, he would

The Making of Modern Italy

say: 'I'll go and be a colonel in Russia or Austria rather than yield and show weakness.' And he gave orders that students should be sent away from Naples, because they were full of new ideas, liable to get excited and quick on the draw. Immediately many poor young men were chased out at top speed. But everyone's irritation, curses and complaints were so great that the order was revoked. Could a government last long which knew neither how to be consistently bad nor consistently good? ...

11 February 1848 The multitude, without going into the matter further, started rejoicing as soon as it heard that the new law constituting the government had been published. They went to the front of the royal palace, and, although it was pouring with rain, they demanded to see the King and salute him. He appeared on the grand balcony. ... Words cannot indicate the emotions we felt at hearing many humble people shouting: '*Viva Italia*! We are Italians!' That word 'Italy', which had at first been uttered by a few and in secret, which had been heard only by a handful, and which had been the last sacred word uttered by so many honourable men as they died – to hear it now uttered and shouted by the people made me feel a tingling run down my spine and through my body, and constrained me to tears.

From *Memoir of my Life* by L. Settembrini (1879)

Charles Albert and *Italia Farà Da Sé*: 1848–9

C King Charles Albert in full *ancien régime* regalia

D This verse about Charles Albert circulated widely in 1847 as the King hesitated and vacillated

In *diebus illibus* [olden days], in Italian lands
The old great parchment tells it all,
A king so maddened by his nurse's milk

That he passed his days in swaying on swings.
A rare case, I'd say, among Kings.
So what did they call him? King Swing the First.

Biagio pushed first, Martino then,
One pushed fast, the other slow,
And slow or fast the King crowed out,
Bravo Biagio, Martino bravo.

Swing there, swing here, what a delicate thing
To dandle-O, dandle-O in the lap of a swing:
Faster – a little – less now - now more,
Sway there, sway here, sway up, sway down.

A popular verse by Domenico Carbone

E   After the granting of the *Statuto* in 1848 commemorative kerchiefs like this were produced. Many are displayed in the Museum of the Risorgimento in Turin, where Charles Albert is presented in a heroic light

Charles Albert and *Italia Farà Da Sé*: 1848–9

F   A table to illustrate economic conditions in Venice before the 1848 revolution

Year	Wheat price (Austrian lire)	Maize price (Austrian lire)	Number of silk workers employed	Amount of tax collected (florins)
1845	16.22	10.61	639	616 000
1846	18.56			619 000
1847	31.92	24.49	410	602 000

From *Nationmaking in Nineteenth-Century Europe* by W. Shreeves (1984)

G   This Revolutionary Catechism is typical of the propaganda circulating among Italian soldiers in Austrian regiments

Q Are you Italians?
A We are by the Grace of God.
Q What does it mean to be Italian?
A It means to be born on Italian soil, of an Italian mother, by an Italian father.
Q What is the distinctive exterior sign of an Italian?
A It is hatred of the German tyrant, hatred which must show in the face, in the bearing, in our words and actions.
Q What are the distinctive interior signs of Italians?
A They are three: memory, intellect and will. ...
Q What are the articles of the creed?
A There are five: First: I believe firmly in the imminent, irrepressible regeneration of Italy. Second: I believe that Italy has all the elements necessary to raise itself to a lasting and powerful level of nationality. Third: I believe that the unification and nationality must be a fount of riches, of power and happiness ... Fourth: I believe in the apotheosis of all those who encounter suffering and death for the redemption of Italy. Fifth: lastly, I believe that the Italians must, can and wish to do everything by themselves.

H   Radetzky reports from Milan to the Austrian government

Yesterday the fighting continued with great intensity and there must have been many casualties on both sides. I am still unable to give an account of my losses for I lack all details. The streets have been pulled up to an extent you can hardly imagine. Barricades close them by the hundred, even by the thousand. The revolutionary party is moving with a caution and cleverness which make it obvious that they are being directed by military officers from abroad. The character of this people has been altered as if by magic, and fanaticism has taken hold of every age group, every class, and both sexes. Yesterday morning I withdrew all troops in the city to the citadel, leaving only those barracks with which we can still keep in touch.

From a report by Radetzky, 21 March 1848

I An Austrian officer tries to explain the high rate of desertion from his Venetian regiment

Daily, hourly almost, the revolution won ground in all provinces, which were denuded of troops and administered by weak or treasonous officials. In all the places through which the transport [of reserve troops] passed, the royal officials had been dismissed and had been replaced for the most part by the most enthusiastic supporters of the overthrow of the existing order. The priests displayed the worst attitude of all and placed themselves with incredible insolence at the head of the revolutionary movement. It was they who were most responsible for inciting and influencing the lowest classes, in particular the peasants. All symbols of imperial authority were destroyed and in their place was planted the tricolour Italian flag. In all places the men of the transport were received with shouts of joy and shouts of *Viva Italia, l'indipendenza, Viva Pius IX*, etc. The richest people, as well as the beggars, the bishops as well as the meanest monks were all wearing the Italian cockade. The men, as native sons, were everywhere given bread and wine and there were even inns where they were given food and drink free.

From a report to the Commander of the 26th Infantry Regiment, 5 April 1848

J Standing on a café table in St Mark's Square, Manin proclaims the Venetian Republic on 22 March

We are free, and we have a double right to boast of it because we have become free without shedding a drop of blood, either our own or our brothers', for I call all men brothers. But it is not enough to have overthrown the old government; we must put another in its place. The right one, I think, is the republic. It will remind us of our past glories improved by modern liberties. We do not thereby mean to separate ourselves from our Italian brothers. Rather we will form one of those centres which must bring about the gradual fusion of Italy into one. *Viva la Repubblica! Viva la Liberta! Viva San Marco!*

K The Pope urges Italians not to fight for unity

Seeing that some at present desire that We too, along with the other princes of Italy and their subjects, should engage in war against the Austrians, We have thought it convenient to proclaim clearly and openly, in this solemn assembly, that such a measure is altogether alien from our counsels, inasmuch as, ... We reach to and embrace all kindreds, peoples, and nations, with equal solicitude of paternal affection. ... We do urgently warn and exhort the Italian people to abstain with all diligence from the like counsels [schemes for unity], deceitful and ruinous to Italy herself, and to abide in close attachment to their respective sovereigns, of whose good will they have already had experience, so as never to let themselves be torn away from the obedience they owe them.

From the Allocution of Pius IX, delivered on 29 April 1848

L   After the reoccupation of Milan Carlo Cattaneo wrote a bitter account of how middle-class 'lackeys' had sacrificed freedom to 'an illusion of military power'

The prophets of liberty should not have remained seated and silent, almost like neutrals or foreigners, and without protest allowed servile ambition to outweigh the safety and glory of the nation. In their hearts they fornicated with royal power; they had more confidence in it than in the strength of the people in which they professed to trust. They betrayed eternal principles for the plate of lentils held out to them by material power. ... They agreed to a pact which put the war of the people in proxy to the court and in payment they gave the mercenary the jewel of liberty.

From *The Milan Revolution of 1848* by C. Cattaneo (1848), translated by Robert Murray

M   Desperately, Daniele Manin urges the Venetian assembly to vote for union with Piedmont

The enemy is at our gates, counting our divisions. Let us give him the lie. Let us forget all parties today. Let us show that today we are neither royalists nor republicans but that we are all citizens. To the republicans I say –- the future is for us. All that has been done or is being done is provisional. The decision belongs to the Diet at Rome.

From a speech by Manin, 4 July 1848

N   The British Foreign Secretary comments sympathetically from the sidelines as events unfold in Italy but shows no wish to become involved in the struggle for independence

15 June 1848 I cannot regret the expulsion of the Austrians from Italy. I do not believe, Sire, that it will diminish the real strength or impair the real security of Austria as a European Power. Her rule was hateful to the Italians, and has long been maintained only by an expenditure of money and an exertion of military effort which left Austria less able

The Making of Modern Italy

to maintain her interests elsewhere. ... The Alps are her natural barrier and her best defence. I should wish to see the whole of Northern Italy united into one kingdom, comprehending Piedmont, Genoa, Lombardy, Venice, Parma and Modena.

31 August 1848 The real fact is that the Austrians have no business in Italy at all, and have no real right to be there. ... We do not wish to threaten; but it is the part of a friend to tell the truth, and the truth is that Austria *cannot*, and *must not*, retain Lombardy; and she ought to think herself well enough off by keeping Venetia, if, indeed that province is really advantageous to her.

28 December 1848 I heartily wish that Italy was *piu forte* [stronger]; but weak as she is, a contest single-handed with Austria would only lead to her more complete prostration, and I doubt whether France is as yet ready to take the field in her support. I do not wish to see Italy emancipated from the Austrian yoke by the help of French arms, but perhaps it would be better it should be so done than not done at all; and if it were to be done at a time when England and France were well together, we might be able to prevent any permanently bad consequences from resulting from it. But the great object at present is to keep things quiet; to re-establish peace in Northern Italy, and to trust to future events for greater improvements.

23 September 1849 The present moment is the moment of reaction in Europe. The Revolutionists have had their swing; the tide is turned, and the Absolutists are for the time in the ascendant. But this state of things cannot last.

Lord Palmerston to the King of Belgium, Lord Ponsonby, Lord Abercromby and his brother

O   Settembrini describes the conflicts which arose after the revolution in the Kingdom of Naples

The gravest preoccupation was Sicily, which rejected the Neapolitan Constitution of February 10, and replied that it still wanted its own Constitution of 1812, desiring to be an entirely separate and independent kingdom. ... These conditions seemed harsh not only to the King, but to a good many Neapolitans and Italians, who said and put in print that Sicily, in separating herself from Naples, would separate herself from Italy; that this 'Sicilianism' was unworthy, an ancient rancour between Palermo and Naples; ... that two constitutions would separate the two peoples more than the sea and for ever. ... The revamped Ministry could not stop the excitement from daily growing. They broke up the great machinery of the old government, but with little wisdom. They got rid of the bad, but they often failed to find the good to put in their places. ... Everybody chatted, in the streets they complained of everything. They had won a constitution by shouting, so everyone thought he could get a job by shouting. ... The masses said: 'And if there is no work, and we are starving, what liberty is that? Previously the King was one man, and ate for one; now they are a thousand, and they eat for a thousand. We must also look to our own situation.' In the provinces the peasants invaded and divided between them the lands belonging to the Crown, or to the landlords who had earlier taken them over and were hated because they had got rich through usury and extortion. ... At the end of March, the whole Ministry, being unable to ride the tempest, resigned without having done any permanent good.

From *Memoir of my Life* by L. Settembrini (1879)

P His most recent biographer summarises Mazzini's address to the assembly soon after his arrival in Rome in March 1849

He called on Romans to take this chance of showing how patriotism was not hostile to religion. They should also show the outside world that freedom and equality could coexist in their republic. Liberty of conscience and speech were rights to be enjoyed by everyone, and there should be no intolerance, no hatred of political opponents, only a united effort to win national independence. Quoting Oliver Cromwell he urged his hearers to 'put your trust in God and keep your powder dry'. They should invite monarchist Piedmont as well as republican Venice and Florence to unite in a joint effort to end the Austrian occupation of Italy.

From *Mazzini* by Denis Mack Smith (1994)

Q An English poet, who was living in Rome during the siege, describes the atmosphere there

Mazzini is a less fanatical, fixed-idea sort of man than I had expected; he appeared shifty and practical enough. He seemed in excellent spirits; and generally confident and at ease. He asked me if I had seen anything of the pillaging which the English papers were acquainted with; he said that any of the English residents would bear witness to the perfect tranquillity, even greater than before, which prevailed in the city (and certainly I see nothing to the contrary). Assure yourself that there is nothing to deserve the name of 'terror'. The worst thing I have witnessed has been a paper in manuscript put in two places in the Corso, pointing out seven or eight men for popular resentment. This was done by night; before the next morning a proclamation was posted in all the streets, from (I am sure) Mazzini's pen, severely and scornfully castigating such proceedings.
[He also describes an incident when confessional boxes were dragged

from a church for use as barricades and Mazzini ordered them to be taken back]

From *Letters and Remains* by Arthur Hugh Clough (1865)

R Mazzini explains why the Roman Republic fought so fiercely

To the many other causes which decided us to resist, there was one intimately bound up with the aim of my whole life – the foundation of our national unity. Rome was the natural centre of that unity, and it was important to attract the eyes and reverence of my countrymen towards her. ... It was therefore essential to redeem Rome; to place her once again at the summit, so that the Italians might again learn to regard her as the temple of their common country. ... The defence of the city was therefore decided upon; by the assembly and people of Rome from a noble impulse and from reverence for the honour of Italy; by me as the logical consequence of a long-matured design.

From the *Life and Writings of Mazzini* (1869)

S The left-wing republican soldier, Carlo Pisacane, gives his explanation for the failure of revolution in 1848–9

Whether ruled by a King, a President or a Triumvirate, the people's slavery does not cease unless the social system can be changed. ... These governments should have translated into action the idea that had brought people together; but each interpreted its mission from a partial viewpoint, and the people were thus divided; they fought but were beaten; and so it happens when the destinies of a nation are directed by individuals without there being any single idea or principle among the masses to indicate the road ahead.

From *The Wars Fought in Italy in 1848–9* by C. Pisacane (1850–1)

Questions

1. Do you think that source A is an 'attempt to arrest the course of events' (as claimed by Hales, the biographer of Pius IX) or a call for a united Italy (as claimed by contemporary nationalists)? **(5 marks)**
2. Compare the impressions given of King Charles Albert in sources C–E. **(5 marks)**
3. Evaluate explanations for the success of revolutionaries in the early months of 1848 in sources B and F–J? **(8 marks)**
4. How adequately is the subsequent failure of the revolutions explained by sources K–O and S? **(7 marks)**
5. To what extent do sources P–R bear out Denis Mack Smith's opinion that 'Mazzini governed with wisdom, moderation and unexpected administrative capacity'? **(5 marks)**

6 CAVOUR AND THE LEADERSHIP OF ITALY: 1849–58

In 1848 the writer John Ruskin wanted to continue his study of Venetian art and architecture but his visit to the city was delayed by reports of revolution, starvation and cholera. When he and his young bride, Effie, did reach northern Italy in October 1849 they found many signs of the recent troubles and the current military occupation. The monastery in Milan containing Leonardo da Vinci's *Last Supper* was being used as a barracks; the new railway bridge at Venice was out of action; the inns were full of Austrian officers 'paying nothing'; the people, wrote Effie, 'are very unhappy'. 'I am a thorough Italian here and hate oppression', she declared, trying to ignore the Austrians. However, neglected by her studious husband and flattered by the attentions of the handsome officers 'in their white coats and light blue Italian trousers', she soon took a kinder view of the occupation. The resentment of Venetian people did not diminish. [A]

All over Italy restored rulers clamped down on their unhappy subjects. Martial law continued in the Austrian dominions and French troops remained in Rome. In Naples, the central duchies and the Papal States some of the many political prisoners were executed to instil terror into the rest of the population. Despite foreign disapproval the repression was not relaxed, except in Lombardy and Venetia where in 1857 Radetzky's stern rule gave way to a more conciliatory administration. Pius IX was now so illiberal that Gioberti changed his mind about an Italian federation led by the Pope. He suggested that Piedmont should champion national unity, though he doubted whether King Victor Emmanuel II and his politicians were equal to the task. [B–D]

Gioberti singled out Piedmont for leadership because of its unique freedom from foreign control and its parliamentary form of government, which had no parallel in Italy. Piedmont's new King was a boorish young man, more interested in military than in parliamentary matters. But the constitution survived the difficult post-war years under the leadership of the trusted d'Azeglio, though he had been seriously wounded in the war. [E–H]

The ablest member of his cabinet was Camillo Cavour, the wealthy businessman and journalist, who was now Minister for Economic Affairs. By 1851 Cavour had reorganised the national finances, reduced tariffs and made commercial treaties with France and Britain (among other countries) – all of which made Piedmont more prosperous. But in that year he withdrew his support for d'Azeglio's moderate conservative government and formed an association (*connubio*) with a centre–left group, awaiting an opportunity to replace the Prime Minister. This came in 1852 when d'Azeglio resigned after a disagreement with the King, who appointed Cavour as his successor. He kept the position until his death nine years later. Though not completely trusted, he was widely admired for his intelligence, self-confidence, dedication to work and ability to get things done. [I–K]

Commerce, industry and agriculture continued to flourish during the 1850s, assisted by more free trade measures and by the construction of roads and railways. However, the standard of living did not improve for the 98 per cent of the population who had no vote. Most people still lived on maize or chestnuts, and every year some died of starvation. No laws were passed to control child labour or to improve prison conditions (which were similar to those in Naples), though Cavour was embarrassed by such abuses and intended to remedy them when he had time. He also hoped that, eventually, the 'dirty' and 'unenterprising' island of Sardinia would catch up with the rest of the kingdom. One radical change he did effect was to shut down many of the kingdom's rich monasteries and confiscate their property. In this instance, though, he was opposed by the King, who did not want to upset the Pope; to save his political life, Cavour compromised. He allowed monks and friars an income for life. For all its limitations and difficulties, parliamentary government survived and Piedmont stood out as the most progressive Italian state. [L]

Piedmontese citizens were freer than other Italians to express their opinions. Many republican exiles lived peacefully in Turin and in 1856 a group of them formed the National Society. Its leaders were Manin (who remained in Paris despite assurances that he would be safe in Turin), Giorgio Pallavicino from Lombardy and Giuseppe La Farina from Sicily. It even included Garibaldi, who had been refused permission to land at Genoa in 1849 but was now allowed into Piedmont on condition that he gave up his radical views. The Society saw its role as educating public opinion rather than organising revolution. Its moderate aim was to create, not an ideal republic, but a country led by the House of Savoy. [M–N]

Among the Society's recruits were former followers of that obdurate revolutionary Mazzini, whose insurrections repeatedly failed. In 1853 he directed a rising in Milan which resulted in many arrests and 50 executions. Even more disastrous was the encouragement he gave to Carlo Pisacane, who sailed from Genoa in 1857 to foment a socialist uprising in Naples. Hostile Neapolitans opposed the small revolutionary band, which was easily crushed by the Bourbon army.

Cavour and the Leadership of Italy: 1849–58

Pisacane committed suicide to avoid being taken prisoner and the Risorgimento lost one of its most intelligent leaders. Not surprisingly, many Mazzinians concluded that Italy was unready for revolution. [O]

Cavour did not need convincing of this. He abhorred revolutionary aims and methods, and alerted governments when he discovered plots like those of 1853 and 1857. Yet he secretly instructed his agents in Tuscany and Modena to stir up unrest and in 1856–7 he turned a blind eye to Mazzini's conspiratorial residence in Genoa. One motive for this double game could have been a hope that the revolutionaries would discredit themselves by their activities. But Cavour also needed evidence that Italians were eager to be liberated because he was trying to attract the backing of Britain or France for a renewed war against Austria. This was no easy task. British governments were sympathetic to Italy's only parliamentary state but did not want to alter the balance of power. France's self-made Emperor, Napoleon III, was tempted to seek glory by engaging in wars but had little time for democracy.

Cavour sought to win the good opinion of the western powers in various ways. To the delight of his own bellicose sovereign, he supported British and French forces during the Crimean War, even though his country's interests were not directly involved. Piedmont gained prestige through one successful engagement and won a seat at the Paris conference table in 1856. Although he persuaded Victor Emmanuel to trim his extravagant moustaches for the occasion and provided generous hospitality to his allies, Cavour gained nothing from the negotiations. [P]

In the following year, however, discreet reports began to reach Cavour that Napoleon III might be prepared to fight Austria. Cavour promptly modified his liberalism to suit his autocratic neighbour; newspapers were suppressed and parliamentary debates were curtailed. Surprisingly the Emperor decided to assist Piedmont after Felice Orsini, an Italian nationalist, made an attempt on his life in January 1858. It is not clear whether he was stirred most by Orsini's impassioned justification for his action, by fears of further assassination attempts or by visions of a new Napoleonic era in Italy. Anyway, in July 1858 the Emperor met Cavour secretly at the French spa town of Plombières. They agreed that France would take part in an early war against Austria and give her blessing to an enlarged Piedmont, which would form part of a loosely united Italy presided over by the Pope. In return, Cavour pledged Savoy and (probably) Nice to France and Victor Emmanuel's pious 15-year-old daughter, Clotilde, to the Emperor's cousin, Prince Napoleon, a notorious middle-aged philanderer. It only remained to find a pretext for war. [Q–S]

Cavour's motives are as mysterious as those of his devious ally. He may simply have wanted revenge for Piedmont's humiliating defeat in

The Making of Modern Italy

the 1848–9 wars, in which his own nephew had been killed. Perhaps his main aim, as nationalists always suspected, was the aggrandisement of Piedmont. It is even possible that Cavour, who had seen very little of the peninsula, yearned to unify Italy.

A Effie Ruskin writes to her mother about Venetian sensibilities
4 January 1852 My Italian music master ... is such a good little man and very clever. ... He says very simply that I will play music in Heaven some day because I am *Buonissina Signora* [fine lady], but he is in horror when I come to play with my black dress lined with orange – the Austrian colours.
16 February 1852 [during carnival week] Masked people were walking [in St Mark's Square] in single file to music. ... They spoke and threw bonbons – but the mob pressed them so much that they could hardly walk. I thought it a very melancholy spectacle and no fun as the people are sulky about it & it is all done by the Governor to promote good feeling and gaiety during the Carnival without success. The crowds were immense but all of the lower classes & quantities of little boys whistling and making a din through wooden penny whistles.

From Effie Ruskin's letters to her mother

B The British ambassador to Turin has similar impressions
From the reports which have been made to me by persons who have had the opportunity of studying this point I believe that one feeling of deep-rooted hatred of the Austrian name pervades the minds of every man, woman and child throughout Lombardy; and that this feeling has immensely increased since the reoccupation of the provinces. ... The people may be kept down by force of arms and military despotism, but Austria will not obtain the affections of the inhabitants or render the Lombard provinces a source of wealth or power to the Imperial Crown.

From a report by Lord Abercromby to Palmerston, 26 January 1849

C The British politician, William Gladstone, visited Naples in 1851 for the sake of his daughter's health and was shocked by what he discovered about the treatment of 20–30 000 political prisoners. His published letters to his party leader, Lord Aberdeen, gained a wide circulation
Now, how are these *detenuti* [detainees] treated during the long and awful period of apprehension and dismay between their illegal seizure and their illegal trial? The prisons of Naples, as is well known, are another name for the extreme of filth and horror. I have really seen something of them, but not the worst. This I have seen, my Lord: the

official doctors not going to the sick prisoners, but the sick prisoners, men almost with death on their faces, toiling upstairs to them at that charnelhouse of the Vicaria, because the lower regions of such a palace of darkness are too foul and loathsome to allow it to be expected that professional men should consent to earn bread by entering them. As to diet, I must speak a word for the bread that I have seen. Though black and coarse to the last degree, it was sound. The soup, which forms the only other element of subsistence, is so nauseous, as I was assured, that nothing but the extreme of hunger could overcome the repugnance of nature to it. The filth of the prisons is beastly. ...

[Gladstone draws attention to the case of Settembrini]

He was capitally convicted in February, though through an humane provision of the law the sentence was not executed; but he has, I fear, been reserved for a fate much harder: double irons for life, upon a remote and sea-girt rock: nay, there may even be reason to fear that he is directly subjected to physical torture. The mode of it, which was specified to me upon respectable though not certain authority, was the thrusting of sharp instruments under the fingernails.

From *Two Letters to Lord Aberdeen* by W. E. Gladstone (1851)

D   An article in the *Spectator* reports from Rome that 24 political prisoners were put to death in a 'homicidal ceremony' between 28 September and 2 October 1852

How They Do Justice in Rome

The conduct of all the prisoners in the presence of death was such as to mark them out for men of courage and firmness. There appears to be no exception. The only traces that remain of the words which they bequeathed to their countrymen are those of encouragement. Simoncelli died singing the *Marseillaise*; another of the prisoners left a message to his friends to defend their country against her enemies. ... But if the case of Simoncelli is multiplied by the number of his colleagues in death and imprisonment at Sinigaglia, it may be multiplied indefinitely by the future slaughters of which this may be supposed to be the first. We may expect the same fate, with the same secrecy, and the same certainty that if amongst their number some few may have been 'guilty' of high treason, many also will be really innocent of any crime whatsoever. The object is terror. ... Such is the fate to which the people are condemned by the dominant influences in the Roman States.

From the *Spectator*, 30 October 1852

E Disillusioned by the events of 1848–9, Gioberti places his hopes in the House of Savoy rather than the papacy

Ecclesiastical Rome loathes the national and civil principle, and so she cannot be the pivot of the Italian Revival, as she was of the Risorgimento [by which he means the period before 1848]. ... In the course of the Risorgimento, the work of direction was divided between Rome and Piedmont, the latter's duties consisting principally of the use of arms and political guidance. Now that the ideal impulse of the ecclesiastical city has failed and the secular city is again oppressed, the double task belongs to Piedmont, which must be both the arm and the brain of the nation. ... The Sardinian monarchy, which until now has been aristocratic, provincial and little favoured by people of ability, must become as progressive, democratic and national as possible. ... Piedmont has only one way of achieving hegemony and success: to proclaim the national unity of Italy and open up the path to its creation by force of arms.

From *The Civil Revival of Italy* by V. Gioberti (1851)

F Queen Victoria records her impressions of her 'Royal brother', Victor Emmanuel, who visited London in 1855 with strict instructions from Cavour to restrain his normal coarse language

He is so frank, open, just, straightforward, liberal and tolerant, with much sound good sense. He never breaks his word, and you may rely on him, but wild and extravagant, courting adventures and dangers, and with a very strange, short, rough manner. ... He is shy in society, which makes him more brusque, and he does not know (never having been out of his own country or even out in Society) what to say to the number of people who are presented to him here. ... He is more like a Knight or a King of the Middle Ages than anything one knows nowadays.

From a letter to King Leopold of Belgium, 5 December 1855

Cavour and the Leadership of Italy: 1849–58

G A drawing of Victor Emmanuel from Queen Victoria's sketch-book [made after the King had cut ten centimetres off his moustache]

H The French ambassador, like Queen Victoria, could write more frankly about the King than could his own subjects

King Victor Emmanuel is in no sense liberal: his tastes, his education and his whole habit of behaviour all go the other way. He tells everyone that 'my father bestowed institutions on the country which are quite unfitted to its needs and the temper of its inhabitants.' To some people he will add, 'but my father and myself have both given our word, and I will not break it.' To others, however, he will say confidentially, 'I am waiting only for the *right moment to change everything*. That moment will be the outbreak of war. Whenever it comes, I shall be ready.' ... Victor Emmanuel, I repeat, does not like the existing constitution, nor does he like parliamentary liberties, nor a free press. He just accepts them temporarily as a kind of weapon of war.

From Baron de Butenval to his Foreign Minister, 16 October 1852

The Making of Modern Italy

I This picture suggests what caused Cavour to write: 'In my social position there is nothing so much to be dreaded as obesity, for it will make me look ridiculous'

J A pen-portrait of Cavour by his close friend, Castelli
His easy manners, his joviality, his genuine interest in new acquaintances, the affability with which he welcomed all who called on him, and his readiness to listen to serious men or any enterprising project, made him popular with all acquaintances as well as intimates. He was respected and loved by his juniors and servants. ... His perceptiveness, his benevolence, his instinctive understanding of our times made him a believer in political and civil equality. Yet deep down you could sometimes find traces in Count Cavour of a less progressive man. ...

From the outset I had set myself to study his real character and to clarify the distrust in which he was held. More than once I showed him the apparent contradictions between what he said and what he did. He would be taken aback for a moment and usually ended up by turning the matter into a friendly joke, realizing that he was in the wrong. ...

His activity was ceaseless; if he was not doing something, he was thinking; hence his occasionally abstracted manner, his odd forms of posture, his constant need to be at work.

From *Count Cavour: Memories of Michelangelo Castelli* (1886)

K   Cavour sums up his own political philosophy in a letter written from Paris

I was undecided for a long time between these contrary directions. Reason held me to moderation: infinite longing to punish our reactionaries thrust me toward Movement; finally, after much agitation and oscillation, I ended by placing myself, like a pendulum, in the *juste-milieu* [middle way]. So ... I am an honest *juste-milieu*, wishing, waiting, working for social progress with all my power, but determined not to purchase it at the price of a general upheaval, political and social. My state of *juste-milieu* does not stop me from hoping for the soonest possible emancipation of Italy from the barbarians who oppress her, nor accordingly from foreseeing that a crisis of at least some violence is inevitable; but I want that crisis to be as restrained as the state of things allows, and I am sure that the fanatic efforts of the men of movement will only delay it and make it riskier.

From a letter written by Cavour in 1835

L   Cavour persuades Parliament to raise taxes and risk a deficit in order to subsidise a transatlantic steamship

You have spent millions upon the new railways of Novara and Susa during the last year. This year you have been still more daring. You have sanctioned schemes for the two most perilous and difficult railways in Europe: you have voted ten millions for new roads in Sardinia. ... After this, will you stop before the expenditure of some hundreds of thousands of lire? After having spent hundreds of millions to make Genoa one of the great commercial centres of Europe, will you refuse to assure to her the commerce of America? ... You will, I hope, give your vote for one further step on the road you have hitherto trodden; a road full of difficulties, surrounded by obstacles and not devoid of dangers, but one which, if we follow with energy, prudence, wisdom, and firmness, will for certain lead this courageous nation to noble destinies.

From a speech to the Senate, July 1853

M Daniele Manin urges fellow nationalists to work with Cavour
Cavour is extremely able and is well known abroad. It would be a grave loss not to have him as our ally, as it would be a grave danger to have him as our enemy. I think we must not overturn him but urge him on. We must work incessantly to form public opinion, because as soon as opinion is clear and forceful, Cavour I am sure will follow it. ... I think Cavour to be too intelligent and too ambitious to refuse the Italian enterprise if public opinion demands it strongly enough.

From Manin to Giorgio Pallavicino, 27 September 1856

N The National Society states its 'noble and holy aim'
We want to unify Italy so that all her vigorous efforts can be concentrated on liberation. We want to reconcile and harmonise the ideas of her intellectuals, as we want to secure a common programme of action; we want concord between provinces, between her cities and classes. We will not repudiate the aristocracy if they recognise our present needs, as we also embrace the common people so long as their pretensions do not go beyond justice and equity. We want concord and tolerance between all sincerely held religions. On the one hand we support the Piedmontese government, for it has a warlike army, money, credit, reputation, and an organised administration; but Piedmont must be ready to work with the Italian people, who have the numbers, the force, the revolutionary zeal, and the inalienable right to override any treaty and become free and independent. Hence we want concord between the dynasty of Savoy and Italy, so long as the former whole-heartedly supports the cause of Italian independence. We accept support from anyone as long as they put Italian independence and unity first.

From the Political Creed of the National Society, 1858

O Pisacane always scorned such 'expedient remedies'
I believe that socialism alone – not the French systems which are all full of that monarchical and despotic idea which prevails in that nation, but the socialism expressed by the formula *Liberty and Action* [Mazzini's motto] – is the one not too distant future of Italy, and perhaps of Europe. ... I am convinced that Italy will be free and great or else a slave. ... It will be a disaster if the people content themselves with vain promises and so make their own fate depend on the will of others.

From *Essay on Revolution* by C. Pisacane (1857)

Cavour and the Leadership of Italy: 1849–58

P In justifying Piedmont's participation in the Crimean War Cavour outlines a different way forward for Italy

Experience of the past years and even centuries has shown how little Italy has benefited from all her revolutions, plots and conspiracies. Far from helping her, they have been one of the greatest calamities that have afflicted this fair land. ... Now, gentlemen, I believe that the first condition for the betterment of the state of Italy ... is to raise her reputation, to act so that all the nations of the world, both governors and governed, render justice to her qualities. But for this two things are necessary: first to prove to Europe that Italy has the political sense sufficient to govern herself properly, to school herself in liberty, that she is in a condition to be able to adopt the most perfect form of government known; and secondly, to show that her military valour is equal to that of her ancestors. You have ... shown by your conduct for the last seven years that the Italians know how to govern themselves with wisdom, prudence and loyalty. There lies before you an equal, if not a greater, service; it is for our country to show that the sons of Italy can fight with true valour on the field of glory. I am certain, gentlemen, that the laurels our soldiers will win on the battlefields of the East, will do more for the future of Italy than all those who have thought to regenerate her with the voice and with the pen.

From a speech to Parliament, 3 February 1855

Q From his prison cell Orsini (awaiting execution following his attempt to assassinate the Emperor) appeals to various sides of Napoleon III's character

As a simple individual I dare to raise my feeble voice from prison, to beg you to give Italy again the independence that Frenchmen helped her to lose in 1849. Let me remind Your Majesty that Italians, including my own father, cheerfully shed their blood for Napoleon the Great, wherever he chose to lead them; and they were loyal to the end. Let me also remind you that neither Europe nor Your Majesty himself can expect tranquillity until Italy is free.

Do not scorn the words of a patriot on the eve of his execution. Deliver my country, and the blessings of 25 million people will go with you for ever.

From a statement by Orsini, 11 February 1858 (which was published in the official gazette in Turin at the end of March)

R Cavour summarises for his army chief, General La Marmora, the very long report on the Plombières agreement which he had already sent to King Victor Emmanuel

1 That the State of Massa and Carrara would be the cause or pretext

The Making of Modern Italy

of the war [i.e. discontented areas ruled by the repressive Duke of Modena who had the backing of Austria].
2 That the purpose of the war would be to drive Austria out of Italy: the establishment of the kingdom of Upper Italy composed of the whole valley of the Po and of the Legations [Romagna] and the Marches.
3 Cession of Savoy to France. That of the County of Nice undecided.
4 The Emperor is confident of the cooperation of Russia and the neutrality of England and Prussia. ...

The only undefined point is that of the marriage of the Princess Clotilde. ... I remain convinced that he [the Emperor] lays very great importance on the matrimonial question, and that on it depends, if not the alliance, then the final outcome. ... I have written strongly to the King not to risk the finest undertaking of modern times out of sour aristocratic scruples.

From Cavour to La Marmora, 24 July 1858

S   The young princess resigns herself to her fate
I have already thought a great deal; but my marriage to the Prince Napoleon is a very serious thing, and one which above all is quite contrary to my hopes. I know too, my dear Count, that it could, perhaps be advantageous to a nation like ours and above all to the King my father. ... I hope Our Lord will guide me with His infallible sustainment; I am placing everything in His hands for now and I cannot decide anything. We will be able to see afterwards.

From the Princess Clotilde to Cavour, 15 August 1858

Questions

1 How useful are the various English viewpoints represented in sources A–D as insights into the state of Italy after the revolutions of 1848–9? **(5 marks)**
2 To what extent do sources F-H suggest that the hopes placed by Gioberti in the Sardinian monarchy [E] were justified? **(4 marks)**
3 To what extent do sources I–L justify the confidence expressed by Manin [M] in Cavour's abilities? **(6 marks)**
4 Compare the different approaches to Italian unification represented in sources N–P. **(5 marks)**
5 What light is shed on the Plombières agreement by sources Q–S? **(5 marks)**

7 NAPOLEON III AND THE UNITING OF NORTHERN ITALY: 1859–60

In 1859 Baron Hübner, the Austrian ambassador to Paris, had an unhappy New Year: at a reception on 1 January Napoleon told him ominously that 'our relations are not as good as they were'. Ten days later Victor Emmanuel II opened a new session of the Piedmontese Parliament with a speech (already vetted by the French Emperor) declaring that he was not insensitive to 'the cry of grief that comes to me from every part of Italy'. These two public utterances heralded the signing of the secret treaty between France and Piedmont, a step towards implementing the plan hatched at Plombières to provoke Austria into declaring war on Piedmont. [A]

Over the next three months all Cavour's energy and guile were devoted to bringing about what Professor Blumberg calls a 'carefully planned accident'. Cavour had to contend with Victor Emmanuel's indiscretions, Queen Victoria's fears, Hübner's attempts at conciliation and Napoleon's constant vacillations. In April Cavour actually threatened to blow out his brains when France joined Britain in trying to persuade Piedmont and Austria to disarm and negotiate. Hübner concluded from this change of tack that the Franco-Piedmontese alliance had lapsed and advised his government to demand Piedmont's demobilisation. When Piedmont rejected the ultimatum war broke out, on 26 April. Napoleon III thereupon followed in the footsteps of his uncle and led 120 000 French troops across the Alps. [B–C]

The state of the Piedmontese army, commanded by a brave but inexpert Victor Emmanuel, showed that Cavour's military preparations had been less successful than his political machinations. Only 60 000 of the promised 100 000 troops were mustered, though 20 000 volunteers flocked to the cause of independence from other parts of Italy. The soldiers were badly equipped, not even having enough maps to guide them through Lombardy. Thus they failed to arrive at Magenta where the first battle was fought on 4 June. (The only Italians who fought were those in the Austrian army.) The French defeated the Austrians and pursued General Guilay's troops across Lombardy to gain a further victory at Solferino on 24 June. The Piedmontese did take part in this battle but with little success. In order to share in the victory the King ordered a subsequent attack on the neighbouring village of San Martino but this was less glorious than Italian paintings suggested. According to the French Minister of War, the Piedmontese were 'ill disposed, ill commanded and fought ill'. These battles were waged in baking summer heat which encouraged the spread of typhus, increased the sufferings of the wounded and hastened the putrefaction of the dead, who lay unburied on the battlefield for days. [D–F]

While Cavour was struggling to keep abreast of the war (a task made harder by Victor Emmanuel's determination to exclude 'mere civilians' from military matters), he was also observing the patriotic revival of central Italy, in the hope that it might be turned to Piedmont's advantage. Since the beginning of the year he had worked with the Turin-based National Society to stir up anti-Austrian feeling in the duchies, being careful always to stress the need for 'unity' and 'independence' rather than 'liberty' and 'revolution'. Events did not always go according to plan. The enormous crowds which gathered in Florence on 27 April were not organised by moderate National Society members like Baron Ricasoli but by a radical baker called Guiseppe Dolfi, whose followers were 'bold and tough working-class men'. But somehow the provisional government, set up after Grand Duke Leopold's hasty abdication and escape to Vienna, excluded the radicals. It was led by Ricasoli, a noble Tuscan who at first wanted to retain autonomy for his region. But the euphoria produced by the war (as well as fear of further revolution induced by Mazzini's arrival in Florence) soon convinced him that Tuscany's best interests would lie in fusion with Piedmont. He may also have wanted to increase the market for the fine Chianti wines produced on his vineyards. Anyway his new conviction was encouraged by the watchful Cavour. [G–I]

After the departure of Austrian garrisons to fight in Lombardy, the Habsburg dukes of Parma and Modena fled and the people of Romagna revolted against the Pope. The National Society members who in May took charge of the new provisional regimes were quick to seek annexation by Piedmont. For the time being Cavour diplomatically declined their request. In July further popular risings occurred in the Marches and Umbria but here the Pope managed to reassert his control, with the help of 2000 Swiss Guards. [J]

These developments in central Italy made Napoleon III suspect Cavour of planning to exceed the terms of their treaty by taking over the region. This suspicion probably played a part in his unexpected decision to make a truce with Austria on 8 July. The disproportionately high human and financial French losses also weighed with him. He was worried, too, that Prussia would come to Austria's rescue and that France would lose the glory it had won. Historians continue to debate which factor was uppermost in Napoleon's mind as he signed the Peace of Villafranca. This left Venetia in the hands of Austria and made no mention of Savoy and Nice, which Piedmont kept even though they had been promised to France. Victor Emmanuel had probably known

Napoleon III and the Uniting of Northern Italy: 1859–60

about the truce beforehand though he claimed to be as shocked about it as Cavour, who went purple with rage and resigned his post, claiming that all his efforts had been wasted. [K–N]

He returned to office in January 1860, by which time Piedmont's position had improved. Lombardy had been incorporated into the kingdom, the people of central Italy gave every sign of wanting Victor Emmanuel as their sovereign and Britain's Liberal Government was led by Italophiles like Palmerston, Gladstone and Lord John Russell. Napoleon III's attitude to Piedmont's further aggrandisement remained in doubt. He had proposed an international congress to discuss the whole 'Italian Question' but had then undermined it by suggesting that the Pope's loss of Romagna was final. Now it looked as though neither papal nor Austrian representatives would attend. [O–R]

The congress never met. In secret negotiations Cavour and the French Emperor agreed that the future of the central regions should be determined by plebiscites – as long as plebiscites also took place in Savoy and Nice. The confidence which both parties had in the outcome of open popular ballots proved justified. In March a vast majority of Tuscan, Parmesan, Modenese and Romagnan males voted – in piazzas festooned with green, white and red – to be annexed to Piedmont. This Kingdom now encompassed more than a third of Italy and nearly half its population. Then, in April, 85 per cent of Savoyard and Niçois citizens, watched over by French troops, voted to become part of France. [S]

For all the public rejoicing, there was much criticism of this bargain. Victor Emmanuel mourned the loss of his transalpine territories. Cavour himself hoped for an opportunity to regain them and still coveted Venetia. Garibaldi, who had been born in Nice, expostulated that it had been sold 'like a rag to the foreigner'. He resumed his old friendship with Mazzini and sought to unite Italy in his own way. An even more implacable opponent of the new arrangements was Pius IX, who excommunicated all who had consented to the dismembering of the Papal States and feared for the remainder of his realm. [T]

While not all Italians felt that they had benefited from Napoleon III's response to their 'cry of grief', it can hardly be denied that he played a vital role in the unification of Italy. [U]

A A Milanese nobleman remembers the bellicose atmosphere of January 1859

News of Victor Emmanuel's speech to Parliament came to Milan the very day it was spoken. I was at the Theatre Della Scala; and all at once I noticed people talking to one another in an excited way, and at the same time I perceived an air of surprise on the faces of the Austrian officers and functionaries. The nervous tension that was in the air and in us all was to break out a few evenings later in the same theatre. The opera *Norma* was given, and the Druids had scarcely begun to sing the chorus of *'Guerra! Guerra!'* ['War! War!'], when the whole house rose up. The ladies waved their handkerchiefs, and all, with one voice and one cry, shouted *'Guerra! Guerra!'*. The chorus was repeated again and again, amid frantic enthusiasm. The Austrian officers who, as usual occupied the front rows of the stalls, did not at first understand the reason for this outburst. They looked inquiringly to the boxes where General Guilay and several of his officers sat. ... Guilay gave the signal, as he struck his sword against the floor. ... The theatre was soon surrounded by troops, and General Guilay departed in the midst of his staff and officers, as if they were banded in his defence.

From *Memoirs of Youth 1847–1860* by G. Visconti Venosta (1900)

B   Queen Victoria writes to French Emperor, using words suggested by the Conservative Prime Minister, Lord Derby
I cannot refrain from taking this opportunity of expressing confidentially to your Imperial Majesty my deep anxiety for the preservation of the peace of Europe, nor can I conceal from myself how essentially that great object must depend upon the course which your Imperial Majesty may be advised to take. Your Majesty has now the opportunity, either by listening to the dictates of humanity and justice, and by demonstrating unmistakably your intention to adhere strictly to the faithful observance of Treaties, of calming the apprehensions of Europe, and restoring her confidence in your Majesty's pacific policies; or, by permitting yourself to be influenced by the ambitions and designs of others, of involving Europe in a war, the extent and termination of which can hardly be foreseen, and which, whatever glory it may add to the arms of France, cannot but interfere materially with her internal prosperity and credit.

From a letter written on 4 February 1859

C   Cavour exercises his persuasive powers on the Emperor
I flatter myself that Your Majesty will know how to frustrate all the attempts of your enemies to prevent you from accomplishing the noblest of all tasks. Your wisdom, your prudence, your moderation, and the loftiness of your ideas, will together recover the support of public opinion which may have momentarily wavered. Austria has misjudged you and adopted a menacing or even provocative tone. She is playing the role of aggressor. And this makes me hope that before long she will commit one of those *aggressive acts* which will justify your armed intervention. I hope so with all my heart.

Napoleon III and the Uniting of Northern Italy: 1859–60

[He writes more frankly to his secretary, Nigra, who was in Paris]
I have written to the Emperor to dissuade him from this Congress idea. I avoided threats and declamation, but I tried to be as positive as possible. ... I hope that we avoid the Congress, for I cannot see where it would lead us. How the devil could we then start a war? ... If only he would give up his fears and begin fighting!

From letters written by Cavour, 19 March 1859

D *Tuscan Troops Saluted at Montechiaro by French Troops Wounded at Solferino* **(1859) by Telemaco Signorini [see front cover]**

E **The war also inspired the poet, Elizabeth Barrett Browning, who lived in Italy and was devoted to the cause of unification**

Now, shall we say
  Our Italy lives indeed?
And if it were not for the beat and bray
Of drum and trump of martial men,
Should we feel the underground heave and strain,
Where heroes left their dust as a seed
Sure to emerge one day?
And if it were not for the rhythmic march
  Of France and Piedmont's double hosts,
  Should we hear the ghosts
Thrill through ruined aisle and arch,
  Throb along the frescoed wall,
Whisper an oath by that divine
They left in picture, book and stone,
  That Italy is not dead at all?

From *Napoleon III in Italy* by E. Barrett Browning (1860)

F **Henri Dunant, a Swiss tourist, describes the aftermath of Solferino. His account led to the formation of the Red Cross**

When the sun rose on the twenty-fifth, it disclosed the most dreadful sights imaginable. Bodies of men and horses covered the battlefield; corpses were strewn over roads, ditches, ravines, thickets, and fields; the approaches of Solferino were literally thick with dead. ... The poor, wounded men that were being picked up all day long were ghastly pale and exhausted. Some, who had been the most badly hurt, had a stupefied look as though they could not grasp what was said to them; they stared at one out of haggard eyes, but their apparent prostration did not prevent them from feeling their pain.

The Making of Modern Italy

Others were anxious and excited by nervous strain and shaken by spasmodic trembling. Some, who had gaping wounds already beginning to show infection, were almost crazed with suffering. They begged to be put out of their misery, and writhed with faces distorted in the grip of the death-struggle. ... Anyone crossing the vast theatre of the previous day's fighting could see at every step, in the midst of chaotic disorder, despair unspeakable and misery of every kind. ... Looters stole even from the dead, and did not care whether their poor wounded victims were still alive. The Lombard peasants seemed especially greedy for boots, and wrenched them ruthlessly off the swollen feet of the dead.

From *A Memory of Solferino* by J. H. Dunant (1862)

G Cavour warns the Piedmontese representative in Florence about the dangers of revolutionary demonstrations

I exhort you and *charge you to use all your influence to prevent street demonstrations* and above all to avoid a collision with the troops of the Grand Duke. The former are almost always useless, and especially so now: in the great enterprise for which Italy is preparing, it is desirable that we shun the errors of 1848 and 1849, among which, and not least, ought to be numbered the disorderly shouting of multitudes. Once the push has been given, it is very difficult to hold back the most enthusiastic. Making a tumult becomes a habit, and those who are brought up to it come to think that with their slogans and their processions they have made a sufficient offering of courage, perseverance and sacrifice.

From a letter written by Cavour to Boncompagni, 20 March 1859

H The *Times* correspondent in Florence reports on the Tuscan revolution

27 April 1859 Bands of soldiers and citizens paraded the streets singing patriotic songs and mingling the names of Victor Emmanuel and Italian independence. ... At an early hour this morning the people (to the number of 20,000) assembled in the Piazza Santa Maria Antonia. Here the tricolour of Italy was raised amid rapturous acclamations, and bands of men of all classes ... dispersed themselves in every direction, each troop led by a bearer of a standard. ... Amid a thousand *vivas* and the waving of banners the Sardinian Ambassador presented himself to the people, reminding them that the eyes of Italy and Piedmont were upon them, exhorted them to respect religion, law, and property, and recommended discipline to the army, quiet and order to all. ... He next announced that the Grand Duke had declared his intention of abandoning

Napoleon III and the Uniting of Northern Italy: 1859-60

Tuscany ... and trusted that the citizens would obey the Government that should be organized to meet the present emergency. ... The most important fact was the perfect command which the leaders of the people seem to possess over each and all. They might be seen going from group to group recommending order and tranquillity. Throughout the entire day no single act of turbulence occurred as far as I have been able to discover.

From a report in The *Times*, 3 May 1859

I   ***The 26th of April 1859*** **by Borrani – a young woman is sewing a tricolour flag. The ironic title suggests foreknowledge of the Tuscan revolution planned for 27 April**

The Making of Modern Italy

J   Odo Russell, the British Agent at Rome, reports to his uncle, the Foreign Secretary, on less peaceful events in the Papal States
24 June The Pope sent Signor Latanzi, a lawyer of repute, to Perugia for the purpose of admonishing the inhabitants to return to their duties and surrender to His Holiness. Unfortunately while Signor Latanzi was still negotiating with the provisional government and before his mission was over, Colonel Schmidt at the head of about four thousand Swiss troops, who had been sent from Rome for that purpose, attacked the town on 20 June. The Perugians at once broke off the negotiations entered into with Latanzi and though insufficiently armed made a desperate resistance. After three hours combat and considerable losses they were compelled to yield to the Swiss. These latter are reported to have lost two Captains, one Lieutenant and about sixty men killed and wounded. I regret to inform your lordship that the Papal soldiers after entering the town acted with great ferocity. They shot everyone they could find and entering private houses pillaged and murdered their peaceful inmates including old men and helpless women, nine of whom were mothers.
1 July Cardinal Antonelli [the Pope's Chief Secretary] told me this morning that he hoped I had not believed the exaggerated accounts which were circulating in Rome respecting the conduct of Papal soldiers at Perugia. ... The Cardinal said that revolutions must be put down and bloodshed was the natural consequence of such a conflict; ... and the fury of the soldiers could not well be controlled at first, which was after all but natural.

From letters to Lord John Russell in 1859

K   A table to show relative losses in the war of 1859

	Killed Officers	Killed Troops	Wounded Officers	Wounded Troops	Missing or taken prisoner
French	196	2 430	863	16 191	1 128
Piedmontese	49	961	233	4 689	1 268
Austrian	169	5 247	944	25 085	19 306
Totals	414	8 638	2 040	46 085	21 702

From *Magenta et Solferino* by R. Bougerie (1993)

L   The French politician, Thiers, an opponent of the Emperor, gives his explanation for the Peace of Villafranca
Napoleon had gained enormously by Magenta and Solferino ... but the *peace* disappointed everyone. He did not choose to confess that his rash advances had put the army into a situation of great danger, from which he could extricate himself only by asking for an armistice.

He assigned as the ground of the peace his fears of Prussia – a motive offensive to our pride. Then Piedmont, which had been his slave, took the bit into her mouth; began to annex without consulting him; persevered in opposition to his orders, his threats, and at last his entreaties; and raised on our south-eastern frontier a formidable power which threatens to increase. He could not control the movement which he had set in motion. ... I know that what he saw of actual war disgusted and alarmed him. He has not had experience enough to be callous to its horrors; scenes frightened him to which his uncle would have been indifferent.

From *Conversations with Thiers* by N. W. Senior (1878)

M Although Victor Emmanuel claimed that Napoleon had treated him 'like a dog' over Villafranca, he admitted to the British military attaché that he was not wholly unhappy about the Peace

His Majesty seemed to own that a great deal had been done but is doubtful as to whether in its present shape the treaty would be a guarantee against another war. This was however more said with the tone of misgiving and real anxiety that it should be otherwise than with any appearance of menace or satisfaction. ... His Majesty talked of Count Cavour who had that day tendered his resignation. I think he was much disturbed at it although professing that it was of no importance now: 'He is a bungler who is always pushing me into some hornets' nest or other; he is mad; ... he gets mixed in follies like this rising in the Romagna and God knows what else. ... His time is up.'

From a report by Lord Cadogan to Lord John Russell, 14 July 1859

N Elizabeth Barrett Browning would not countenance any criticism of her hero, Napoleon III

Well, now let me speak of our Italy and *the peace*. 'Immoral', you say? Yes, immoral. But not immoral on the part of Napoleon who had his hand forced; only immoral on the part of those who by infamies of speech and intrigue (in England and Germany) brought about the complicated results which forced his hand. Never was a greater or more disinterested deed intended and almost completed than this French intervention for Italian independence; and never was a baser and more hideous sight than the league against it of the nations.

From a letter to Anna Jameson, 26 August 1859

The Making of Modern Italy

O   Central Italy was deluged with propaganda on the merits of fusion with Piedmont – even pastries displayed the King's features. Verdi's music continued to be a source of inspiration and his name took on a special significance as an acrostic for *Vittorio Emmanuele Re D'Italia*

P   Some observers, like the French representative in Tuscany, felt that more sinister tactics were being used

Then followed great pressure from the Piedmontese Government on the Tuscan Government. No blood was shed, there was no disorder evident, because there was no resistance. But the current of the unionist idea dragged the uncertain along with it, submerged the frightened and cut itself a huge bed, exerting a fascination on people's minds by its very success.

 I saw some strange recantations emerge from informed and important men. ... Baron Ricasoli has been the inflexible and unscrupulous agent of this regime of terror, and there is good reason to be surprised ... that in his last report to M. Boncompagni he should praise the freedom and spontaneity of the municipalities' votes in favour of annexation – since nearly a hundred magistrates have been deprived of office and replaced by people of his own persuasion, and several municipal councils ... resigned the day after their vote in protest against the violence to which they had been subjected.

From Marquis de Ferrières to the French Foreign Minister, 18 May 1859

Napoleon III and the Uniting of Northern Italy: 1859–60

Q The British Foreign Minister gives his blessing to the proposed annexations

Tuscany, Modena and Parma have deposed their Sovereigns, who had previously quitted their dominions for foreign countries. Romagna has declared against the temporal power of the Pope. However unfortunate for these Sovereigns the position in which they have been placed may be, we have to deal with a state of things which actually exists. ... [These provinces], one and all, have proposed annexation to Sardinia. Their National Assemblies have voted that annexation, and their governments are now carried on in the name of Victor Emmanuel. So far as the opinion of Her Majesty's Government is concerned this solution would be perfectly satisfactory. In our view, it would be desirable, for the sake of France and Austria, of Italy and Europe, that a strong Monarchy should exist in the north of Italy, not continually trembling for its independence, and not looking to a powerful neighbour for support.

From Lord John Russell to the British Ambassador in Paris, 26 November 1859

R The Pope appeals desperately to Victor Emmanuel

Do I need to interest Your Majesty himself in assuming the sacred duty of protecting and sustaining the rights of the Holy See. Certain it is that when I reflect upon what is going on in Romagna, where they are making laws, governing, taking part of the goods of the Church, and committing many other arbitrary acts, all in the name of Your Majesty, I am bound to apply myself to interesting you in favour of the Patrimony of the Church, which is oppressed and despoiled in Your Name. ... The right opportunity is the Congress, and it is there that Your Majesty's name should be brought to bear to declare openly that you will not confiscate the goods of others, and much less a part of the robe of Jesus Christ, which remained whole even on the hill of Calvary.

From Pius IX to Victor Emmanuel, 3 December 1859

S A participant describes the Tuscan plebiscite

The polling has been going on for two days. The countryside has been *en fête*, and everybody has hastened to vote. ... There was never any sign of violence, and if anybody says he was not free to give his vote he is either a brazen-faced liar or a great coward. ... The peasantry are thought to have voted as their landlords told them to, but this will have been the only instance of coercion. Some landlords have contented themselves with making them vote, while leaving them free to vote whichever way they liked. Others, the majority, handed out to their tenants ballot papers which were marked 'Union with Piedmont'. In Pescia, Giorgio Magnani said to his men: 'Those that don't vote won't drink.' The landowners have paralysed the influence of the priests, and this shows that the current revolution derives its strength solely from the aristocracy.

From *Diario 1859–1860* by M. Tabarrini

T   Garibaldi cannot accept the cession of Nice to France
If you reply that Nice has simply been exchanged for two more important provinces [Tuscany and Romagna], it must still be said that any such traffic in peoples is repugnant to every civilised conscience. It would also set a dangerous precedent, and might undermine confidence in the future integrity of our country. The government justifies itself by citing the plebiscite which is due to take place on April 15 and 16. ... But the presence of great numbers of policemen, the flatteries and threats which are continuously being employed, the direct pressure used by the government to force this union with France, ... the absence from Nice of many citizens for one reason or another, the precipitous haste in which this vote is being forced through, all these facts make it impossible to hold a truly free vote by universal suffrage.

From a speech in Parliament, 12 April 1860

U   A modern French historian acclaims Napoleon III
His Italian campaign ... established the principle of nationality as the just basis of states. The right of people to self-determination was recognised and achieved by the practice of plebiscites, though Germany brutally rejected this practice in completing its own unification. Italy was created in two years, after two centuries of vain hopes. ... Napoleon III, a great modern visionary, could not fulfil his mission of civilising Europe, his Latin allies being the first to reject it by their ingratitude.

From *Magenta et Solferino* by R. Bougerie (1993)

Questions

1. With what different feelings do the writers of sources A–C view the possibility of war in Italy? **(4 marks)**
2. Compare the portrayal of the war in the picture (source D), the poem (source E) and the eye-witness account (source F). **(5 marks)**
3. To what extent are Cavour's fears of revolution (source G) borne out in sources H–J? **(4 marks)**
4. Compare the usefulness of sources K–N for explaining the motives behind the Peace of Villafranca? **(5 marks)**
5. In the light of sources O–U, comment on Mazzini's opinion that the new kingdom in Northern Italy was created by bartering peoples and territories. **(7 marks)**

8 GARIBALDI AND THE LIBERATION OF THE SOUTH: 1860

On 27 April 1860 Garibaldi, who was then staying near Genoa, received a telegram from Sicily. It read: 'Offer barrels 160 rum America pence 45 Sold 66 English 47. Expect Lire 114 barrels 147 Brandy without offer. Reply immediately.' Garibaldi had not suddenly become a dealer in wines and spirits; when decoded the message said that the popular revolt in Palermo had collapsed. As a result Garibaldi declared that 'it would be folly' to launch the expedition to Sicily which he and other nationalists had been planning. Yet two days later, hearing that the peasants were still up in arms, he changed his mind. On 6 May he sailed from Genoa with about a thousand volunteers, who were mostly young professionals, students and urban workers from northern Italy. What inspired this risky venture which was so radically to affect Italian history?

Garibaldi had for years dreamed of a 'single Italy' encompassing the whole peninsula. He had supported Piedmont and fought in the war of 1859 but he was not prepared to settle for the North Italian Kingdom formed as a result of Cavour's diplomacy. Furthermore his anger at the cession of his birthplace to France prompted him to win the initiative from Cavour. Once he knew that Sicily was ripe for insurrection, he seized the moment. Furthermore Mazzini was urging him to go – and would have joined the expedition in person had he not been prevented by an attack of lumbago.

Cavour, by contrast, did as much as he could to hinder Garibaldi's departure, though he would not jeopardise his reputation by openly opposing the popular General. Cavour had been unable to prevent the volunteers from gathering in Genoa and collecting money for new rifles. But at the last moment the government made sure that these weapons were locked up in store so that the Garibaldini had to make do with rusty old muskets. Nor did they manage to provision the two paddle steamers which they acquired with much in the way of food, water, coal and ammunition. When Garibaldi put in at the Tuscan port of Talamone to make good these deficiencies and to organise his motley 'army', he confirmed Cavour's worst fears by dispatching a small force to raid the Papal States. Cavour made further efforts to thwart Garibaldi's plans and even spoke of having him 'exterminated'. [A–D]

Nevertheless the Thousand landed safely at Marsala in Sicily on 11 May. Their subsequent conquest of the island, which was defended by

25 000 well-armed Neapolitan troops, astonished contemporaries and still puzzles historians. Eyewitness accounts demonstrate Garibaldi's charisma and tactical brilliance as well as the courage of his followers, who were determined to 'make Italy – or die'. Their numbers were swelled by thousands of poor Sicilians whose 'patriotism' had mainly to do with an age-old desire for independence, to say nothing of hatred for landlords and government officials. For the time being, however, their motives were irrelevant. Their support was a vital factor in Garibaldi's success. [E–F]

On 14 May, after the victories of Calatafimi and Palermo, Garibaldi declared himself Dictator of Sicily in the name of Victor Emmanuel. But the distrustful Cavour was determined to gain control of the situation in the south. First he sent La Farina, leader of the National Society, to Sicily in order to annex the island for Piedmont. Garibaldi resented the interference and expelled La Farina – though he himself was actually finding the Sicilians rather hard to govern. Cavour then put pressure on Francis II, the new King of Naples and Sicily, to grant a constitution; but this did nothing to reconcile his subjects. Next Cavour tried (through agents) to provoke his own moderate and manageable revolt in Naples. This too was a failure, due in part, no doubt, to Cavour's ignorance of the region – he thought its inhabitants spoke Arabic. Finally he tried to prevent the Garibaldini crossing from Sicily to the mainland. However, he was unable to gain the cooperation of Britain, whose Liberal Government was cautiously sympathetic to Garibaldi's expedition and correspondingly suspicious of Cavour, described by Russell, as 'the catspaw of France'. [G–I]

After an unimpeded crossing in mid-August, Garibaldi's soldiers advanced north almost unopposed. The Bourbon King was virtually powerless in the face of widespread adulation for the General, who made a triumphal entry into Naples on 4 September, still in the name of Victor Emmanuel. The 40 000-strong Neapolitan army withdrew to the north of the kingdom, from where it launched an attack a month later. Garibaldi's leadership proved as effective in the defensive battle of the Volturno as it had been in mobile warfare. Though suffering heavy losses (2000 killed, wounded and missing), he spurred his troops on to victory and forced the Bourbon army into a further retreat. [J–L]

By this time it was also threatened from the north – by the Piedmontese troops which Cavour had decided to dispatch after Garibaldi's occupation of Naples. General Cialdini, with the secret connivance of Napoleon III, ruthlessly conquered most of the Papal States, including the Marches and Umbria. But he carefully refrained from attacking the Patrimony of St Peter, the area around Rome which was still guarded by the French. Indeed, it was partly to protect the Holy City from Garibaldi, who had avowed his intention of occupying

Garibaldi and the Liberation of the South: 1860

it, that Cavour had sent the army. He also feared that Garibaldi might fall under the influence of Mazzini and set up a democratic republic in the south. In reality, the volunteers were in no condition to advance to Rome; and so loyal was Garibaldi to Victor Emmanuel that when he heard of the approach of the King's troops he ordered that they should be received 'like brothers'. [M–N]

Now Garibaldi agreed to hold an immediate referendum in Naples and Sicily to determine whether the inhabitants wanted to be part 'of a single indivisible Italy with Victor Emmanuel as constitutional king'. It took place on 21 October and 99 per cent of the voters placed their slips in the 'Yes' boxes. (Similar plebiscites were held a little later in the Marches and Umbria, where, too, enormous majorities voted for annexation.) It only remained for Garibaldi to meet Victor Emmanuel and hand over his conquests; the Garibaldini were disbanded and the General himself, having refused a commission in the Piedmontese army, returned quietly to his farm on Caprera. [O–P]

Garibaldi was now said to be 'the most popular man in Europe' and his island home was inundated with visitors and letters begging for locks of his hair, threads from his shirt or even parings from his nails. After his death he became the subject of a full-blown cult. Historians have revered him too: A. J. P. Taylor called him 'the most admirable man in modern history'. Do his Southern Italian exploits merit these accolades? Plainly his military reputation is well deserved: it is astonishing that his untrained, ill-equipped volunteers gained such decisive victories throughout the campaign. Nor can Garibaldi's patriotism be questioned: he genuinely cared more that Italy should be united than about who did it or what type of regime took charge. It is difficult, too, to find serious fault with his character: vain and humourless he may have been but his incorruptibility, contempt for personal glory and genuine human warmth shine out still.

Whether he deserves his glittering reputation as 'Liberator of the South' is another matter. Historians now consider that, although Garibaldi welcomed the support of the peasants, he was not really interested in their concerns. They wanted the division of communal land, lower taxes and revenge on the landlords; he decreed free trade, conscription and protection of property. He lived up to his name as Dictator, imposing authoritarian rule. In the face of widespread peasant insurrection his government sided with landowners like the Prince of Salina, evoked in Giuseppe di Lampedusa's novel *The Leopard*, whose 'personal privileges had come through all these events battered but still lively'. After Garibaldi's departure many of his followers retreated to the hills and became 'brigands', at war with the old landlords and the new regime. Thus the great liberator can be held partly responsible for the bitter civil war which raged in the south from

The Making of Modern Italy

1861 to 1865, causing more deaths than all the wars of unification put together. His 'gigantic figure', wrote Costantino Nigra, continued to cast its 'enormous shadow' over southern Italy. [Q–R]

A The Piedmontese government decides to obstruct Garibaldi
It was unanimously decided to refuse Garibaldi the guns he requires for the Sicilian insurrection, lest the European capitals should be alarmed, in view of the imprudent publicity given by him and his friends to the preparations he has in hand for Sicily.

From Cabinet Minutes, 24 April 1860

B A young volunteer sets off on Garibaldi's expedition
Parma, 3 May Garibaldi is going and I am going to be one of the fortunate few who will go with him.
At Parma station, 4 May I've counted them! Seventeen in all, mostly students, a few workmen, three doctors. ... They say that in the Romagna train we shall find plenty of comrades, first-rate people.
At sea, 6 May So two ships with the names of two free provinces, Piedmont and Lombardy, are sailing to bring liberty to two slave provinces. ... One hears all the various dialects of north Italy, but it seems that the Genoese and Milanese predominate. By their looks, manner, and speech the greater number seem to be cultivated people.
Talamone, 9 May While we wait for the water, we are served out with arms. My share has been a rusty old gun (what a thing!), a belt like a policeman's, a bayonet, a cartridge pouch and twenty cartridges. But didn't they tell us at Genoa the we should have brand new carbines? ... What shall we do in Sicily so ill equipped?

From *The Diary of One of Garibaldi's Thousand* by Giuseppe Abba

C Cavour telegraphs the Governor of Sardinia
Garibaldi has embarked with 400 volunteers on two steamers for Sicily. If he enters a port of Sardinia, arrest the expedition. I authorise you to employ, if required, the squadron commanded by Count Persano.
[In fact, it seems that Admiral Persano did not interpret this as a serious order]

From Cavour's telegram of 7 May 1860

D Cavour expresses his fears in a letter to Nigra
I regret Garibaldi's expedition as much as anyone. ... I could not stop his going for force would have been necessary. And the Ministry is in no position to face the immense unpopularity which would have been

drawn upon it had Garibaldi been prevented. With the elections taking place, and depending as I do on the votes of every shade of moderate liberal to counter the opposition and get the French Treaty through, I could not take strong measures to stop him. At the same time I omitted nothing to persuade Garibaldi to stop this mad scheme.

From Cavour's letter to Nigra of 12 May 1860

E   Abba describes the Thousand's first battle

Salemi, 14 May The General has ridden through the city on horseback. When the populace sees him they take fire. There is magic in his look and in his name. It is only Garibaldi they want. ... The Sicilian insurgents come in from all sides by the hundred, some on horseback, some on foot. There is tremendous confusion and they have bands which play terribly badly. I have seen mountaineers armed to the teeth, some with rascally faces and eyes that menace one like the muzzles of pistols.

Above Calatafimi, 16 May The hill before us was flashing with arms. It appeared to be covered by at least 10 000 soldiers. ... I saw Garibaldi there on foot with his sheathed sword over his right shoulder, walking forward, keeping the whole action in view. Our men were falling all round him and it seemed that those who wore the red shirt were the most numerous victims. ... The first, second, and third terraces up the hillside were attacked at the point of the bayonet and passed, but it was terrible to see the dead and wounded. Little by little, as they yielded ground, the Royalist battalions retreated higher up. They concentrated and thus grew stronger. At last it seemed impossible that we could face them. They were all on the top of the hill and we were around the brow, tired, at the end of our tether, and reduced in numbers.
[Eventually the 'supreme clash' came and the royalists 'fired their last salvo']

   When the Neapolitans began to retreat under cover of their riflemen I saw the General again watching them with a look of exultation. ... It seemed a miracle that we had conquered.

From *The Diary of One of Garibaldi's Thousand* by Giuseppe Abba

F   A poet who was also part of the Thousand describes the battle for Palermo, which took place at the end of May

There was no sign of any local rising until quite late in the day. We were on our own, eight hundred of us at most, spread out over an area as large as Milan. It was impossible to expect any planning, let alone any orders, but somehow we managed to take the city against 25 000 well-armed and well-mounted regular soldiers. We, on the

The Making of Modern Italy

other hand, were real ragamuffins. ... We ran in ones and twos like sheep, through alleys and squares, chasing Neapolitans, and also to stir up the Palermitans to revolt or at least to make them build some barricades. But we succeeded only indifferently. For the Neapolitans were too busy running away and the Palermitans in seeking refuge from the indiscriminate gunfire which was now taking place. When Palermo finally fell, it had been all our doing, ours alone. Garibaldi showed the very height of courage, and we too were heroes just because we believed in what was strictly impossible. If these were not miracles, then St Anthony is no saint.

From a letter by Ippolito Nievo, 24 June 1860

G La Farina reports to Cavour on the situation in Sicily

Garibaldi is greatly beloved. But no one believes him capable of running a government. In fifteen days these Sicilians have read Garibaldi as if they had known him for fifteen years. No one wishes to wound him, but all are determined not to tolerate a government which is the negation of all government. ... Under such circumstances as these, all eyes are fixed upon me. ... The immediate convocation of the Assembly, to vote the annexation and regulate universal suffrage, is greatly desired. ... Garibaldi is irritated, troubled and weary beyond belief, and his conversation plainly shows that the cares of government are crushing and overwhelming him.

From a letter by La Farina, 10 June 1860

H Abba's experiences in Sicily suggest that the Dictator was not finding it easy to achieve national unity

Parco 22 May [Abba tries to win round a sceptical friar]
  'We want to make one great people.'
  'You mean, one territory; as far as the people are concerned, one or many, they are bound to suffer and they go on suffering and I have not heard that you want to make them happy.'
  'Of course! The people will have liberty and education – '
  'Is that all?' broke in the friar. 'Liberty is not bread, nor is education. Perhaps these things will suffice for you Piedmontese but not for us here.'
  'Well. What do you want then?'
  'War! We want war, not against the Bourbons only, but against all oppressors, great and small, who are not only at court but in every city, in every hamlet.'
Catanisetta 5 July On mustering we find that about fifty of the Sicilians who came with us from Palermo have deserted, some even taking their rifles with them. They are peasants who blaze up like straw and

Garibaldi and the Liberation of the South: 1860

then lose interest. The Council of War condemns them to death. ...
The good ones are townsmen and the Palermitans themselves. They
are civilized, well-intentioned, respectful young men.
Near Mount Etna 15 August Bixio [one of Garibaldi's officers] in a few
days has raged like a tiger through the villages of Etna, where terrible
rioting had broken out. He was seen in one place after another as an
apparition of terror. At Bronte there had been division of property,
arson, vendettas, fearful orgies, and, to cap it all, cheers for Garibaldi!
... The guilty are to be judged by a Council of War. Six of them are to
be executed, shot in the back together with the lawyer Lombardi, an
old man of sixty, who had been the leader of the horrid outburst.
Among those who carried out the sentence were cultured, gentle,
young men in red shirts; doctors, artists and the like. What a tragedy!
After Bronte other villages felt the weight of Bixio's powerful hand.
They called him a savage brute, but they dared not do more. However
far the fortunes of war take us away, the terror of witnessing this
man's tempestuous wrath will suffice to keep the population of Etna
quiet.

From *The Diary of One of Garibaldi's Thousand* by Giuseppe Abba

I   Cavour expresses his mixed feelings about Garibaldi
12 July Garibaldi has become intoxicated by success and by the
praise showered on him from all over Europe. He is planning the
wildest, not to say absurdest, schemes. As he remains loyal to King
Victor Emmanuel, he will not help Mazzini or republicanism. But he
feels it his vocation to liberate all Italy, stage by stage, before handing
her over to the King. He is thus putting off the day when Sicily will
demand annexation to Piedmont, for he wants to keep his dictatorial
powers which will enable him to raise an army to conquer first
Naples, then Rome, and in the end Venice. ... The government here
has no influence over him. On the contrary he mistrusts everybody
whom he imagines to be in touch with us. La Farina has been treated
in a disgraceful way, first isolated, then expelled from Sicily without
the slightest reason.
9 August Garibaldi has done Italy the greatest service that a man
could do: he has given the Italians self-confidence; he has proved to
Europe that Italians can fight and die in battle to reconquer a
fatherland. ... This notwithstanding, it would be highly desirable if a
revolution in Naples came about without him, for that would reduce
his influence to reasonable dimensions. If, in spite of all our efforts, he
should liberate southern Italy as he liberated Sicily, we would have no
choice but to go along with him and wholeheartedly.

From Cavour's letters to Nigra in 1860

The Making of Modern Italy

J   An English traveller witnesses the reception Garibaldi received on the mainland

Reggio, 21 August The population are frantic in their demonstrations of joy. All the men appeared to be armed, and are joining. ... Garibaldi's reception, and that of his troops here far surpasses anything met with in Sicily – there is not near so much noise and demonstration, but much more reality.

Cosenza, 1 September Amid a torrent of cheers, their saviour made his entry – '*Il nostro secondo Gesu Cristo*' being the constant ejaculation with these simple people. Indeed I have been many times told in all sincerity by the peasants, that he is the brother of the Redeemer – a strange contrast to the opinion of the Neapolitan soldiers, who, in obedience to a very common superstition in South Italy, say that Garibaldi has sold himself, body and soul, to the devil. In proof of this, they appeal to his apparently charmed life, adding that the rifle balls merely lodge in his red shirt, and he shakes them out after he done fighting.

Naples ,11 September Not only was all business suspended, but the people roused themselves into a state of frenzy bordering on madness, which oftimes becomes ridiculous, and at others unfortunately dangerous, numerous assassinations taking place. Night and day the entire population were in the streets.

From *The Campaign of Garibaldi in the Two Sicilies* by Commander C. S. Forbes (1862)

Garibaldi and the Liberation of the South: 1860

K A contemporary lithograph of Garibaldi likens him to Christ

L An English woman resident in Naples helps to look after the wounded Garibaldini

Money has been given most liberally, but it gets shamefully thrown away, through the incorrigible thieving propensities of the Neapolitan officials. Baskets full of provisions come in at one door and go out of the other and are re-sold and the money goes into the pockets of the hospital staff. ... It was a barrack turned into a hospital. ... Don't imagine that it has any sanitary arrangement whatsoever; no pipes nor drains; simply the open floor of the room. ... Accustomed as I am to come across the dirt and smell of the streets here, I never imagined the possibility of such an odour.

The Making of Modern Italy

[One day] we found the men looking better than usual; they had had a good night because they had seen the General. ... The only patient who was worse was the nice young fellow who had the great wine-glass-shaped ball through his shoulders. He had been getting on well; but, dear silly fellow, he lost his head with joy to see Garibaldi, and jumped out of bed ... and the wounds broke out bleeding.

From a letter by Harriet Meuricoffre, 8 October 1860

M Cavour justifies sending an army to the south

As the Bourbon government had recognized its own powerlessness by surrendering the town of Naples without a fight, morally it was dead. Should we have allowed the germs of revolution which we had destroyed in northern Italy to multiply elsewhere? No, we could not. By resolutely seizing the direction of political events in southern Italy, the King and his government prevented our wonderful Italian movement from degenerating; they prevented the factions which did it so much harm in 1848 from exploiting the emergency conditions in Naples after its conquest by Garibaldi. We intervened not to impose a preconceived political system on southern Italy, but to allow people there to decide freely on their fate. ... In the Roman States, too, our presence can be equally justified. Even those most considerate of papal rights cannot surely believe that these states under the Pope could go on existing once they found themselves caught between liberal northern Italy and a revolutionary Italy in the south. ... Perhaps the means we adopted to carry out this great act have not been entirely regular; but I do know that the cause of Italy is holy, and the end perhaps will justify any irregularities in the means.

From a speech to the Senate, 16 October 1860

N The Piedmontese General Cialdini issues a stern order

Make it known that I am shooting all peasants caught carrying arms. Quarter will be given only to regular soldiers. Executions have already begun today.

From a telegram to the Governor of Campobasso in the Abruzzi, 24 October 1860

O The English Admiral Mundy (who had cast a friendly eye on the expedition from his ship the *Hannibal*) describes the plebiscite in Naples

22 October Yesterday I visited a few of the polling places in Naples whilst the election was going forward. More than 100 000 people took advantage of the opportunity of recording their opinion. ... Perfect order reigned everywhere; but I think, considering the general temper

100

Garibaldi and the Liberation of the South: 1860

of the inhabitants, it would have required strong moral courage for anyone to publicly announce himself as an enemy to the sacred watchword of '*Italia Una*'. Every man privileged to the franchise had first to produce his paper from the mayor, showing that he was entitled to vote; he was then admitted through a file of the National Militia up to a platform on which the urns were fixed. The urns to the right and left of the central vase had the words '*si*' and '*no*' painted on them respectively in large type. Up to one of these the man had to walk beneath the gaze of a dozen scrutineers, and thrust in his arm and draw out a card.

From *HMS Hannibal at Palermo and Naples during the Italian Revolution* by Sir Rodney Mundy (1863)

P   One of Garibaldi's aides watches him meet Victor Emmanuel
26 October The King talked of the fine weather and of the bad roads, interrupting the conversation to administer gruff reproofs and manual checks to his restless horse; then they rode on ... but soon each returned to his centre – in one line the modest redshirts, in the other the splendid uniforms shining with gold, silver, crosses and medals. ... Meanwhile the clash of arms, the shining plumes and helmets, had attracted all the peasants of the environs, who hailed Garibaldi with their usual enthusiasm. He was at his wits' end to direct attention from himself to the King, and keeping his horse a few paces behind, he cried, with an imperious gesture, 'This is Victor Emmanuel, the King, your King, the King of Italy. *Viva il Re!*'

The peasants stared and listened: then not understanding the tenor of his speech, again shouted, '*Viva Garibaldo!*'

From *The Red Shirt: Episodes* by Alberto Mario (1865)

The Making of Modern Italy

Q   In this Italian cartoon entitled *The Worship of Garibaldi,* (1863) Napoleon III, Pius IX and Ratazzi (who became Prime Minister after Cavour's death in 1861) try to snuff out the candles lighted for 'Saint' Guiseppe Garibaldi

Garibaldi and the Liberation of the South: 1860

Questions

1 What do sources A, C and D suggest about Cavour's feelings towards Garibaldi's expedition? **(6 marks)**
2 How useful are sources B, E and F in explaining the difficulties and advantages experienced by Garibaldi during the expedition of 1860? **(6 marks)**
3 On the basis of sources G–L assess the extent of support for Garibaldi's rule among southern Italians. **(8 marks)**
4 How useful are sources M–P in explaining why southern Italians voted to come under the rule of Victor Emmanuel? **(6 marks)**
5 How apt a comment is source Q on Garibaldi and his influence? **(4 marks)**

9 BISMARCK, PIUS IX AND THE INCLUSION OF VENICE AND ROME: 1861–71

In January 1861 parliamentary elections were held throughout most of the Italian peninsula, but only literate men over the age of 25 who paid 40 lire a year in taxation could vote. So two per cent of the population chose the moderate conservative legislature, led by Cavour, which assembled in Turin and was duly opened by Victor Emmanuel, now bearing the title King of Italy. Some regretted that the new nation was not the democratic republic of which Mazzini had dreamed, or the federation of Italian states envisaged by Gioberti, or even a dictatorship like Garibaldi's in southern Italy. But most were prepared to settle for Piedmont's constitutional monarchy as established in 1848. [A]

The first country to give official recognition to united Italy was Britain. In fact, Russell had sent a despatch as early as October 1860 welcoming Victor Emmanuel's extended rule. But the Queen stopped him from following this up with a circular to the Great Powers expressing a hope that the cities of Venice and Rome, 'so thoroughly Italian in their character', should share the same 'good government' as Italy. Congratulations on the Italian achievement came also from Prussian liberals, who longed for a German Cavour. But Otto von Bismarck, the conservative Prime Minister of Prussia appointed in 1862, had no particular interest in Italian unification. It is ironic, then, that in his ruthless pursuit of a united Germany Bismarck should have helped to bring Venetia and Rome into the Italian Kingdom. [B–C]

Although Victor Emmanuel's first speech from the Italian throne did not mention Venetia or Rome, there is no doubt that many Italians shared Garibaldi's indignation at their exclusion from the kingdom. But since the Austrian Emperor and the Pope had strong forces with which to defend their last Italian possessions, it was hard to see how Italy could acquire them without foreign help. Cavour tried to persuade Napoleon III to complete his task of 1859; but the French Emperor was in an awkward position. He sympathised with Italians' desire to expel Austria but could not risk French lives again for that cause. On the other hand, he dared not upset his Catholic subjects by removing French troops from Rome. [D–F]

Another faint hope in 1861 was that the Pope might voluntarily relinquish his temporal power in return for a guarantee of the Church's complete independence in spiritual matters. Cavour was working towards such a compromise when, in June, he suddenly died

Bismarck, Pius IX and the Inclusion of Venice and Rome: 1861–71

of malaria at the age of 51. Pius IX, though generous enough to say a Mass for the repose of Cavour's soul, was adamant in rejecting his proposal as well as similar ones put to him in 1862 through English intermediaries. [G–J]

Cavour's successors as Prime Minister (of whom there were seven before 1870) were no less anxious to solve the 'Roman Question'. Reason having failed, they lent an ear for a time to Garibaldi's passionate cry of '*Roma o morte*' ['Rome or death']. In the summer of 1862 the King and the Prime Minister, Urbano Ratazzi, allowed Garibaldi to gather an army of 2000 volunteers in Sicily and cross to the mainland. But caution then prevailed and government troops attacked the Garibaldini at Aspromonte. This fiasco resulted only in an increased adulation for Garibaldi, who never fully recovered from being wounded in the foot, and in the resignation of Ratazzi, who was now disowned by the King. [K]

In September 1864 a new Prime Minister, Marco Minghetti, tried a more conciliatory approach when he signed an agreement with Napoleon III. French troops would be withdrawn from Rome within two years, provided that the Italian capital was moved from Turin to Florence. The Emperor seems to have thought that this transfer would quieten the clamour for Rome but most Italians continued to see the Eternal City as their true capital. The Pope, no longer having to please Paris and now placing his 'trust only in God', issued his famous *Syllabus of Errors*. This condemned all forms of liberalism and toleration as the 'false doctrines of our unhappy age'. [L–M]

By 1866 there had been no progress towards the 'redemption' of either Venice or Rome. Europe was now more concerned with Bismarck, who had already fought a victorious war against Denmark and was preparing to challenge Austria for the leadership of Germany. As part of that plan he allied with Italy in April; Venetia would be Italy's reward for fighting Austria if war broke out within two months. Both Prussia and Italy were confident of victory but Napoleon III was worried that Austria would win and return in triumph to Italy. So he signed his own agreement with Austria, promising his neutrality in return for Venetia, which he would then hand over to Italy. Secret though this treaty was meant to be, the Italian Government now realised that it would gain Venetia whatever happened. Nevertheless, when fighting began in June, Victor Emmanuel was eager to lead his troops into battle. He wrote, 'The one thing which truly gives me pleasure is fighting wars.' [N]

The King's military prowess had not improved since 1859. Thanks largely to his confused strategy and lack of preparation Italian forces performed disastrously in this war, retreating at the battle of Custoza on 24 June from a smaller Austrian force. But, on German soil, Prussia

The Making of Modern Italy

won such a decisive victory at Königgrätz on 3 July that Austria immediately gave up Venetia to France in order to be able to withdraw troops from Italy. Once they had left, Victor Emmanuel's soldiers, together with Garibaldi's omnipresent volunteer army, occupied most of Venetia as well as the Southern Tyrol, which was largely Italian-speaking. The King also ordered a belated naval attack on the Austrian fleet at Lissa, but this ended in another humiliating defeat. Exasperated with an ally which could not 'make war seriously', Bismarck ended the conflict quickly and Italy had to accept 'a miserable peace'. In a Venice hotel room the French handed over Venetia (excluding the Southern Tyrol) and a plebiscite then confirmed that it was part of Italy. Whatever Victor Emmanuel might claim, Venetians had not been freed by the 'Third War of Independence'. [O–P]

Soon after the Austrian army departed from Venice in October 1866, French troops left Rome in fulfilment of the September Convention of 1864. Their going gave Garibaldi another chance to complete his 'sublime mission'. For a second time the King plotted secretly with Ratazzi (once again Prime Minister) to allow Garibaldi and his forces to invade Papal territory in 1867. However, as the Prussian historian Ferdinand Gregorovius witnessed, the ageing patriot-soldier was let down by the Roman populace which was 'nowhere stirring' and worsted by 'the papal troops who were so derided'. Finally French soldiers hurried back and defeated the Garibaldini at Mentana on 3 November. [Q]

Over the next two years Bismarck prepared to consolidate Prussia's leadership of Germany by making war on France while Pius IX continued his war on liberalism. Both conflicts culminated on the same fateful day. On 14 July 1870, Bismarck was at Ems crafting the telegram which he knew would provoke Napoleon III into declaring war, while in the Vatican bishops and cardinals voted for Papal Infallibility. By the end of the week Napoleon III had announced that his army would soon be 'at Berlin' and Pius IX had declared that the Supreme Ponfiff could never err when pronouncing on 'faith and morals'.

Early in August Napoleon withdrew French troops from Rome to assist their comrades-in-arms on the Prussian frontier. But these reinforcements did not prevent the Prussian victory at Sedan on 2 September or Napoleon's abdication two days later. Italy seized the opportunity which Bismarck had provided. On 20 September the Italian army entered Rome and, after token resistance, Pius IX ordered a white flag to be hoisted on the dome of St Peter's. Rome had become part of Italy. There had been no popular rising, but a plebiscite confirmed that this was what most Romans wanted. [R]

In the Law of Guarantees (May 1871) the Pope was left with the

Bismarck, Pius IX and the Inclusion of Venice and Rome: 1861–71

Vatican and his summer palace at Castel Gandolfo, as well as the promise that the state would not interfere with the Church. But Pius had refused to sign the Law and became a voluntary 'prisoner in the Vatican', his temporal power gone but his spiritual authority enhanced. Most Italians rejoiced as Rome assumed its position as capital. The people's representatives quickly found accommodation in empty palaces and dissolved convents. Victor Emmanuel moved into the Quirinal Palace, formerly a Papal residence, claiming that the 'redemption' of Rome had been willed by God. But Gregorovius could not resist pointing out that the King owed 'everything to fortune and to the achievements of Prussia'. [S]

A A Dutch painting by Tetar Van Elven (1861) commemorates *The Inaugural Session of the First Italian Parliament*

The Making of Modern Italy

B Russell sends a letter which made Cavour cry with joy
There appear to have been two motives which have induced the people of the Roman and Neapolitan States to have joined willingly in the subversion of their governments. The first of these was, that the Governments of the Pope and the King of the Two Sicilies provided so ill for the administration of justice, the protection of personal liberty, and the general welfare of their people, that their subjects looked forward to the overthrow of their rulers as a necessary preliminary to all improvement in their condition. The second motive was, that a conviction had spread since the year 1849 that the only manner in which Italians could secure their independence of foreign control was by forming one strong government for the whole of Italy. ... Looking at the question in this view, Her Majesty's Government must admit that the Italians themselves are the best judges of their own interests. ... It must be acknowledged that the Italian revolution has been conducted with singular temper and forbearance. ... The extreme views of democrats have nowhere prevailed. ... The venerated forms of Constitutional Monarchy have been associated with the name of a King who represents an ancient and glorious dynasty. ... Her Majesty's Government will turn their eyes to the gratifying prospects of a people building up the edifice of their liberties, and consolidating the work of their independence, amid the sympathies and good wishes of Europe.
P. S. You are at liberty to give a copy of this despatch to Count Cavour.

Lord John Russell to Sir James Hudson, Ambassador at Turin, 27 October 1860

C A leading Prussian Liberal casts envious eyes on Italy
If some day a Prussian minister would step forward in the same way and say ... 'I have moved boundary markers, violated international law, and torn up treaties, as Count Cavour has done,' gentlemen, I believe that we will then not condemn him. And if an inexorable fate should carry him off in the midst of his brilliant career, as happened to Cavour, before he achieved his high goal to its full extent, then we will erect a monument to him, as the history of Italy will erect one to Count Cavour, and I do believe that even a soaring ambition will be content with such a monument.

From a speech by Karl Twesten in the Prussian Parliament, June 1861

D Before leaving for Caprera in October 1860 Garibaldi tells the English Admiral Mundy of his true feelings
I shall never rest satisfied till emancipation from foreign rule has been effected throughout the entirety of the Italian kingdom. Rome and

Venice are not French and Austrian cities. They are Italian cities, they belong to Italy alone and the powerful of the earth have no right to retain them.

From *HMS Hannibal at Palermo and Naples during the Italian Revolution* by Sir Rodney Mundy (1863)

E The new American consul found 'an inconsolable discontent' in Venice, where in 1861 nationalists organised a boycott of any festivities which Austrians were likely to attend

Instead of finding that public gaiety and private hospitality in Venice for which the city was once famous, the stranger finds himself planted between two hostile camps. ... Society is exclusive association with the Austrians or with the Italians. The latter do not spare one of their own number if he consorts with their masters and though a foreigner might expect greater allowance, it is seldom shown him. ... The Venetians are now a nation in mourning and have disused all their former pleasures and merry-makings. Every class, except a small part of the resident titled nobility, seems to be comprehended by this feeling of despondency and suspense. ...

As the Venetians are a people of indomitable perseverance, long schooled to obstinacy by oppression, I suppose they will hold out till their union with the kingdom of Italy. They can do nothing of themselves, but they seem content to wait forever in their present gloom.

From *Venetian Life* by W. Dean Howells (1883)

F Cavour's secretary, Nigra, had now become Ambassador to Paris. He was also something of a poet, as is suggested by this song in which he serenades Empress Eugénie on the boating lake at Fontainebleau in 1863

Lady, if some time on your tranquil lake
The silent Emperor rocks with you,
Tell him that on the Adriatic,
Poor, nude and cadaverous,
Groans and languishes Venice,
But she exists ... and waits.
[The Empress apparently told Nigra that he was wasting his time]

G Cavour proposes a solution to the Roman Question

Rome is the only city in Italy with more than purely local memories; the entire history of Rome from the time of the Caesars to the present day is the history of a city whose importance extends infinitely beyond its own territory, of a city, that is, destined to be the capital of

Italy. ... We must go to Rome, but on two conditions: we must go there in agreement with France; and the reunion of this great city to the rest of Italy must not be interpreted by the great mass of Catholics in and outside Italy as a sign of the Church's servitude. That is, we must go to Rome, but the true independence of the Pontiff must not be lessened. We must go to Rome, but civil authority must not extend its power over the spiritual order. ... I am ready to proclaim in Italy this great principle: a free Church in a free State.

From speeches by Cavour in Parliament, 25 and 27 March 1861

H   A Catholic historian suggests a reason for the Pope's refusal to consider such a compromise
During those very winter months while the conversations were proceeding the Piedmontese pro-consuls, Pepoli in Umbria and Valerio in the Marches, were putting into operation the anti-clerical laws of Turin, and Mancini was extending them, in even more violent fashion, to Naples. ... Cavour allowed and encouraged practices which were bound to ruin the chances of an accord.

From *Pio Nono* by E. E. Y. Hales (1954)

I   The journal of Ferdinand Gregorovius, a Prussian historian living in Rome, conveys the mutual hostility between Church and State in 1860–61
November 29 On October 24, the General of the Jesuits, addressed a protest to Victor Emmanuel, concerning the dispersal and the spoliation of the Jesuit order. It has lost three houses in Lombardy, six in Modena, eleven in the States of the Church, fifteen in Sicily, nineteen in Naples. At present the order of Jesus numbers in all 7144 members.
December 18 All Cavour's proposals for an arrangement have been declined. The Pope remains in Rome; no plan has been formed. ... If the French, as the Romans hope, withdraw their troops, the Piedmontese will enter and the Pope will then leave the city. ... The day before yesterday the police closed the Café Nuovo because a tricolour flag had been found there; and this morning the corners of the streets were covered with the arms of Savoy, which the secret National Committee had stuck up during the night. The police tore them down.
March 21 On the 18th the Pope held an allocution. It is worthy of note in that he herein acknowledges that the Papacy finds itself at variance with modern society, with Liberalism, with progress and civilisation. ... The Pope says that he is asked to become reconciled to modern society and its ideas, and to Italy; but that these insidious proposals

are made with the intention of forcing him to divest himself of all his rights, to sanction a Vandal-like sack of the Church, and to recognise injustice as justice.

From *Roman Journal 1852–74* by F. Gregorovius (1907)

J In July 1862 the British Agent in Rome, Odo Russell, was summoned by the Pope who asked whether he could take refuge in England if forced to leave Rome

I replied that I trusted His Holiness would never have to resort to so extreme a measure and would rather make peace with Italy than abandon Rome. The Pope shook his head mournfully and asked me whether I had read the late declaration of the Bishops and whether I had ever taken the trouble to study the Roman Catholic religion. I replied that I had, but that neither had convinced me of the necessity of the Temporal Power. I believed on the contrary that the Spiritual Power would be far stronger without the temporal millstone round the neck of the Papacy which required the support of a foreign army to impose it on Italy. ...

'My son,' the Pope said, 'the Temporal Dominion was given by God to his Vicar upon Earth. God alone can take it from him. The Lord's will be done.' 'And if events,' I continued, 'deprive Your Holiness of the Temporal Dominion, what then?' 'Then,' the Pope replied, 'I must submit to God's will, but I cannot by any act of my own give up the States of the Church, which I hold in trust. They are not my property, I cannot dispose of them, God must decide whether his Vicar on Earth is to be a temporal sovereign or not.'

From a letter to his uncle, Lord John Russell, 15 July 1862

The Making of Modern Italy

K *Garibaldi Wounded at Aspromonte*. The uniformed figure in the cloak is Colonel Pallavicini, who led Italian troops against the volunteers and fulfilled the 'painful duty' of demanding Garibaldi's surrender. The bandages used on Garibaldi later became 'sacred' relics

L The cabinet debate on 'which city should be the national capital' aroused much interest, according to Gregorovius

September 24 A feverish excitement has laid hold of Italy. ... The majority hope that Florence will be the last halting-place before Rome. I do not believe in a reconciliation with the Papacy, which will never renounce its provinces. The crisis is a great one. Either Cavour's programme will triumph, or the country will fall into anarchy. Victor Emmanuel has risked a desperate stroke in uprooting the monarchy from its native soil. ... Turin is moving convulsively; riots took place on the 20th and 21st; the troops fired, and much blood was shed.

November 13 Florence (which is inundated) prepares to receive the kingdom of Italy, in order through the newly united power to exercise irresistible pressure on Rome. Rome is wrapped in ominous silence, and the clergy wear the sardonic smile of the dying. These days remind me of the history of the Middle Ages.

From *Roman Journal 1852–74* by F. Gregorovius (1907)

M Some of the 80 'errors of our time' condemned in the Papal *Syllabus* of 1864

15 Every man is free to embrace and profess the religion he shall believe true, guided by light of reason.
17 Protestantism is nothing more than another form of the same true Christian religion, in which it is possible to be equally pleasing to God as in the Catholic Church.
55 The Church ought to be separated from the State, and the State from the Church.
76 The abolition of the temporal power, of which the Apostolic See is possessed, would contribute in the greatest degree to the liberty and prosperity of the Church.
80 The Roman Pontiff can and ought to reconcile himself to, and agree with, progress, liberalism, and civilisation as lately introduced.

From the *Syllabus of Errors* (1864)

N Italy is the subject of secret diplomacy

SECRET CONVENTION BETWEEN FRANCE AND AUSTRIA

Article 1: If war breaks out in Germany, the French government undertakes with regard to the Austrian government to keep absolute neutrality and to make every effort to obtain the same attitude on the part of Italy.

Article 2: If the outcome of the war favours Austria in Germany, she undertakes to cede Venetia to the French government at the time of concluding the peace. If the outcome of the war favours her in Italy,

The Making of Modern Italy

she undertakes not to change in this kingdom the *status quo ante bellum* [the situation existing before the war], unless by agreement with France.
Additional Note: In handing over Venetia to Italy, the French government shall stipulate the maintenance of the temporal authority of the Pope and the inviolability of the territory at present under his authority.

From the treaty signed in Vienna, 12 June 1866

O   Gregorovius comments on Italy's performance in the 1866 war

June 20 The Italians will have to stand their trial. They are now a free people, that demand their rights from the world.
June 27 Italy has no military capacity. Since the fall of the Roman Empire the country has only suffered the invasion of foreigners, and has invariably stood on the defensive. At no period has she appeared as the conqueror.
July 8 Prussia gained the decisive victory at Königgrätz; the Austrian army is annihilated. The news arrived at five this evening. At six in the morning the *Observatore Romano* published the despatch with the announcement of the cession of Venice to the French Emperor. The impression made here is indescribable; readers in every street; nowhere a sign of joy. The patriots are humiliated by the thought that Italy is to receive Venice as an alms from the hand of Napoleon, instead of having acquired it by a great national effort.

From *Roman Journal 1852–74* by F. Gregorovius (1907)

P   Odo Russell reacts to the same news, in a letter from Italy

Venetia is to be ceded, Italy is made, a great fact in history! All foreign questions cease for Italy from now. ... Let her prove her goodwill by being the first to disarm and settle down to peace, industry, and commerce and all the rest will come of itself. By the rest, I mean the Pope and Rome. The Pope will have to bend before public opinion, when his French bayonets are gone and the *inexorable logic of facts* will assimilate and absorb Rome, without the interference of men. Everybody one meets has some ingenious or fantastic solution to the Roman Question to propose. My humble advice would be to *do nothing and let the question settle itself*.

From a letter to Lord John Russell, 27 August 1866

Bismarck, Pius IX and the Inclusion of Venice and Rome: 1861–71

Q   A report by another English Liberal, written after Garibaldi's second attempt to conquer Rome, suggests that Victor Emmanuel followed no such advice

I saw many other persons, the burden of whose song was the same, viz. that the king was the great obstacle, that he was ignorant and false, and an intriguer whom no honest man could serve without damage to his reputation. ... Hearing that I was at Florence he sent for me and kept me for two hours. He began by attacking the Emperor [Napoleon III] savagely for his intervention, and upon my asking why the Convention [of September 1864] had not been observed he threw the whole blame upon Rattazzi, who he said had furnished arms, men and money to Garibaldi, and had applied for the assistance of Prussia without his knowledge.
[Victor Emmanuel went on to give his 'solemn assurance' that the September Convention would in future be respected by Italy.]

From a report from Lord Clarendon to Lord John Russell, 1 January 1868

R   In 1870 the Roman Question reaches its climax in the pages of Gregorovius, whose account is not, of course, unbiased

March 10 The Pope is firm as a rock in the conviction that he is predestined by God to place the dogma as a crown on the structure of the hierarchy. He holds himself a divine instrument in the shattered system of the world, as the mouthpiece of the Holy Ghost. I saw him yesterday going about on foot in the Corso, and looked at him closely. He seems to me very fallible, his gait shaky, his complexion pallid. Oh, that such men already dead and buried should continue to darken the world.

August 6 Italy remains neutral. The French are embarking at Civita Vecchia [Rome's port], and Rome will fall as soon as Napoleon is overthrown.

September 23 The Italians entered Rome at 11 a.m. on the 20th. In other circumstances the event would everywhere have produced great excitement; now it is merely an insignificant episode in the great world drama.

October 30 The transformation of the city seems to me like the metamorphosis of jugglery. Italians have replaced the papal troops. ... Every minute flags are hung out, demonstrations made. ... The Pope has announced himself a prisoner and has issued protests. ... The cardinals never show themselves; ... all their pomp and magnificence have ended in smoke. ... Rome will forfeit the cosmopolitan republican atmosphere which I have breathed here for eighteen years. She will sink into becoming the capital of the Italians, who are too weak for the great position in which our victories have placed them.

From *Roman Journal 1852–74* by F. Gregorovius (1907)

The Making of Modern Italy

S **Mazzini, although elected to Parliament, was not allowed back into Italy to take his seat. In 1871 he pronounces his verdict on the events of the last 12 years**

The Italy which we represent today, like it or not, is a living lie. Not only do foreigners own Italian territory on our frontiers with France and Germany, but, even if we possessed Trieste [Trentino] and Nice, we should still have only the material husk, the dead corpse of Italy.

Italy was put together just as though it were a lifeless mosaic, and the battles which made this mosaic were fought for reasons of calculating dynastic egoism by foreign rulers who should have been loathed as our natural enemies. ... The Venetians, despite their heroic defence in 1849, come to us by kind permission of a German monarch. The best of us once fought against France for possession of Rome; yet we remained the slaves of France so long as she was strong. Rome therefore had to be occupied furtively when France lay prostrate at Germany's feet just because we feared to raise our ancient war cry against the Vatican.

The battles fought by Italy in this process were defeats. Custoza and Lissa were lost because of the ineptitude or worse of our leaders. Italians are now a vassal people, without a new constitution to express their will.

From a letter by Mazzini to Guiseppe Ferretti, 25 August 1871

Questions

1. Compare the way in which the new Italy is greeted by foreigners in sources A–C. **(4 marks)**
2. How similar are the Italian emotions conveyed in sources D–F? **(5 marks)**
3. Use sources G–J and L–M to discuss the controversies surrounding the question of Rome becoming the capital of Italy. **(8 marks)**
4. What different methods of gaining Rome and Venetia are shown or suggested in sources K and N–R? **(6 marks)**
5. Assess Mazzini's claim in source S that Rome and Venetia were acquired through 'calculating dynastic egoism by foreign rulers'. **(7 marks)**

10 WHO UNITED ITALY?

Ever since the Kingdom of Italy was declared there have been diverse opinions about how much credit should be given to its various creators.

1 Early Reputations

This section examines how the founders of Italy were viewed at the time of their deaths.

Cavour (died 1861 in Turin)

A Cavour's colleague, d'Azeglio, reacts to the Prime Minister's death
We have all been stunned – that is the right word – by the death of poor Cavour. The news has affected me like one of those blows of Providence, the meaning of which it is impossible to grasp at first. As for him, it is perhaps for the best: to disappear without having fallen – not everyone has such luck. For us it is a terrible ordeal; ... will God be able to save Italy without Cavour? ... It remains to be seen what decision the King will take. Cavour created a vacuum around him; he had agents rather than collaborators; now that he has disappeared there is a whole ministry to create.

From a letter by d'Azeglio, 10 June 1861

B Pius IX abhorred all that Cavour stood for but felt able to forgive him after his death, according to a French diplomat
Suddenly, in a low bass voice, as though he were speaking to himself, without bothering about my presence, he murmured these words: 'Ah! How he loved his country, that Cavour. That man was truly Italian. God will assuredly have pardoned him as we pardon him.'

From *Personal Memories of Pius IX* by H. d'Ideville (1878)

C An Italian MP compares Cavour to Pitt the Younger, who led Britain during the French Revolutionary wars
He was our Pitt. And I would almost add greater than Pitt – for he had all this Englishman's constancy, tenacity, firmness of purpose, and implacable hatred for his country's enemy, and in addition had to

The Making of Modern Italy

struggle against the slenderness of the means that Italy could scrape together. Pitt took action and resisted with a lever called Great Britain; Cavour had only a tiny wedge called Piedmont. But, like Pitt, he made use of that independent dictatorship with which his King and country had invested him – and the results he obtained from it were a hundred times more magnificent. Pitt overthrew a man; Cavour created a nation!

From *The Decline of the Turin Parliament* by F. P. della Gattina (1862)

Mazzini (died 1872 in Pisa where he was living *incognito*)

D   An English historian living in Rome witnesses 'a wonderful demonstration to Mazzini's memory', at which the Italian Government was not represented

The procession along the Corso ... was long and well-organised. It took about three quarters of an hour marching by each point, was accompanied by a bust of Mazzini, and ended on the Capitol [where the bust was placed between those of Michelangelo and Columbus]. The sight was a very surprising one when one thinks that it was done in the very metropolis of Catholicism, in honour of one of Catholicism's bitterest enemies ... and very wonderful, too, considering that Mazzini did it all by his pen from a foreign country.

From letters by Sir Edmund Lecky, 22 and 27 March 1872

E   The Swiss journalist Marc-Monnier felt free to express his admiration for Mazzini only after his death

We can now keep an old promise; we can appreciate for his true worth the man who was the founder of Young Italy, the steadfast defender of national unity, the soldier of Milan, the triumvir of Rome. He was defeated everywhere but never destroyed, always able to recover, spurred on by disillusionment, enriched by defeat, a marvellous example of courage and persistence, and, in spite of his ordeals, ever more faithful and fervent. He could raise legions with a word and throw them into mad adventures where they knew they would die. This man, without a country, without a home, chased from everywhere to take refuge in a distant island, held masses and armies in his hand, and, standing alone against Europe, held her in check and made her afraid.

From *Swiss Review*, 1877

Who United Italy?

F Mazzini's fellow-exile, Antonio Gallenga, does not agree

No man won so many admirers as Mazzini and yet secured so few friends. If we except a few devoted Englishwomen, there is scarcely a human being whom long familiarity had not estranged from Mazzini. With manners consummately affable and courteous he combined an overweening conceit and a narrowness and bigotry of view which hardly tolerated independent minds. He was a lonely genius, all apart from the common ways of other mortals, spurning the suggestions of the plainest common sense, professing to do all for his fellow-beings, yet nothing with them or by their aid.

From an article in *The Times*, 12 March 1872

King Victor Emmanuel II (died 1878 in Rome)

G Italian veneration for the first King of Italy is enshrined in the enormous Victor Emmanuel Monument, built in Rome between 1885 and 1911, dwarfing even the Colosseum

The Making of Modern Italy

Garibaldi (died 1882 on Caprera)

H   A conservative Catholic judges Garibaldi's career
Garibaldi was born among the people. Having no serious education, he had been forced to earn his living as a worker. He then set himself up as a kind of tribune of the people under the auspices of Mazzini. ... Always he gave himself airs as though he were another [George] Washington. ... People lavished excessive praise on him because, in an egotistical world, he himself was not seeking a job, or a decoration, or money. Yet at the same time he could break out easily into vulgar outbursts which upset his friends and which were meat and drink to his detractors. As no one contradicted him, excessive praise only increased his self-esteem. ... Not for this man the ordinary procedures of liberal government. The only methods with which he was familiar were those of armed insurrection. He could destroy, but he did not know how to build.

From *Italian Independence* by Cesare Cantu (1878)

I   Garibaldi's former secretary, Francesco Crispi, is less critical
This is the century of the poor, the century of the common man, and no one better than Garibaldi foresaw this fact and championed the cause of their redemption. ... What one can truthfully admit is that he deeply felt in his own person the sufferings of the working man. ... It was as a dictator that Garibaldi ruled Naples and Sicily and it was this dictatorship which made possible the unification of Italy. ... This was a dictatorship with all the benefits and none of the vices of dictatorship. It witnessed the harmonisation of unlimited executive authority with the wishes of public opinion.

From an obituary of Garibaldi by F. Crispi, 7 January 1882

2 Historical views before 1945

The period of the Risorgimento has been hotly contested among both Italian and foreign historians.

J   Before the First World War liberal English historians like G. M. Trevelyan adopted an optimistic view
Nothing is more remarkable – though to believers in nationality and ordered liberty nothing is more natural – than the stability of the Italian Kingdom. ... The foundations of human liberty and social order exist there on a firm basis. The growing difficulties of the social

problem, common to all Europe, find at least mitigation in the free political institutions of a nation so recently created by the common efforts of all classes. ... In Italy the traditions of the Risorgimento unite and elevate her children. All classes from the king to the workman, all provinces from Piedmont to Sicily are bound together by these memories of a history so recent yet so poetical and so profound.

From *Garibaldi and the Making of Italy* by G. M. Trevelyan (1911)

K   After Mussolini set up his Fascist regime in 1922 liberal Italian historians like Adolfo Omedeo defended the parliamentary government established by the Risorgimento

The men of the Risorgimento acted for the people. They made themselves become the nation, as the seven thousand Israelites ... became the true Israel. But – and this is their great merit – they believed in the people and in the nation. ... They were obsessed by, and felt, their responsibility to edify the people. If no completed work emerged, that is because a people cannot be improvised in fifty years. ... The Italian nation was completely new. But they limited themselves to the structures on which the people and nation could be grafted. ... One must hold firmly to their tradition and their spirit. One cannot abandon and destroy foundations laid with such difficulty.

From *Defence of the Risorgimento* by A. Omedeo (1926)

L   Antonio Gramsci, a Communist writer gaoled by the Fascist Government, subjected the Risorgimento to Marxist analysis

The Moderates [conservative monarchists] belonged economically to the upper classes. ... They were intellectuals and political organisers, and at the same time company bosses, rich farmers or estate managers, commercial and industrial entrepreneurs. They exercised a powerful attraction on the whole mass of intellectuals of every degree who existed in the peninsula, ... to provide for the requirements of education and administration. ... The Action Party [republicans] not only could not have – given its character – a similar power of attraction, but was itself attracted and influenced: on the one hand, as a result of the atmosphere of intimidation which made it hesitate to include in its programme certain popular demands (for instance, agrarian reform); and, on the other, because certain of its leading personalities like Garibaldi had, even if only desultorily, a relationship of personal subordination to the Moderate leaders. For the Action Party to have succeeded at the very least in stamping the movement of the Risorgimento with a more markedly popular and democratic character it would have had to counterpoise to the 'empirical' activity of the Moderates an organic programme of government which would reflect the essential demands of the popular masses, and in the first place of the peasantry.

From *Prison Notebooks* by A. Gramsci (written 1929–35)

M Fascist historians like Gioacchino Volpe were able to fit the Risorgimento into their own version of history

Without betraying either Risorgimento or fascism, we can describe fascism as a new Risorgimento or as an explicit and conscious revival of the Risorgimento after half a century of incubation of the new forces which were weak or absent in the first Risorgimento. ... Think of the manner and degree to which fascism or fascist Italy has found itself in certain representative figures of the Risorgimento, in a Gioberti and a Mazzini, in a Garibaldi and in Cavour himself. Think of the identification of certain aspirations or attitudes. The Risorgimento too felt the need to create that identity between private and public interests, between the individual and the state, in short that unity of life which has been lost. The Risorgimento too, even if its point of departure was liberal aspirations and independence, felt unity, power, greatness as fundamental, even if not as exclusive values. ... But the Italy of the Risorgimento was an Italy without the people. ... The last phase, the phase of the most active and conscious participation of the people in the life of the nation and the state, is that in which we are now living, that of fascism.

From *History of the Fascist Movement* by G. Volpe (1933)

N Some English historians, like Sir James Marriott, also saw the culmination of the Risorgimento in the fascist regime

The attainment of unity and the occupation of Rome ... did not solve all the problems of the young Nation-State. ... Cavour imposed upon Italy a type of Parliamentary Democracy, for which, if not manifestly unfitted by tradition, temperament and training, she was certainly unready. ... A nation, so recently and imperfectly united, needed a period of discipline before it could assume the exacting responsibilities of self-government. ... Italy has [now] found salvation in the acceptance of a popular dictatorship.

From *Makers of Modern Italy* by J. A. L. Marriott (1931)

3 Post-War Reassessment

After the Second World War Italy rejected the descendants of Victor Emmanuel by voting to become a republic. Post-war historians tended to question the heroic, romantic view of Italian unification and to analyse the motives and actions of its leaders more sceptically.

Who United Italy?

O The English historian, Denis Mack Smith, describes the difficulties he encountered when he began his pioneering work

One reason why the division inside the national movement had previously been studied insufficiently was that much of the relevant documentation was barred to scholars, or else had been doctored for political reasons. Such falsification of history was excusable in the early years after 1860 when there was an urgent need to consolidate the not very vigorous sense of national unity and so conceal the strength of internal divisions. But the excuse of political emergency became less valid in course of time. Early in the twentieth century, when the argument was advanced that such concealment had become harmful and even dangerous by obscuring any truthful understanding of some fundamental national problems, Prime Minister Giovanni Giolitti made the discouragingly negative reply that 'it would not be right to let beautiful legends be discredited by historical criticism'. ... This preference for officially sanctioned mythology was the reason why, when in 1946 I visited Italy to study Cavour's political practice, I came up against a courteous but firm opposition from the authorities on the grounds that the material was still 'too delicate' to be consulted.

From the Introduction to *Cavour and Garibaldi* by D. Mack Smith (1985 edition)

P After completing an alternative project on Garibaldi's revolution in the south, Mack Smith gained access to Cavour's correspondence and was able to write his acute analysis of the relationship between these two Risorgimento leaders

On close inspection Cavour and Garibaldi become – probably like most people – at once greater and lesser than first appearances had suggested; and it was in their least generous and least perceptive side, namely their hostile attitude to each other, that they found one of the mainsprings of action with which to create the unitary state. Upon the tension between these two the fate of Italy for a time depended. If Garibaldi renounced caution and set out for Sicily, a decisive consideration with him was his fury at Cavour's sale of Nice, and his conviction that the government could not be stimulated to remedial action except under the stress of imminent danger. When, later on, he sailed across the Straits to Naples, this was partly so that he might defy the French in Rome, and so overturn the Napoleonic alliance upon which Cavour relied. If Cavour then invaded the Marches, this was because he was frightened that the revolution would reach Rome and even penetrate his own kingdom of Sardinia. In January 1861, Cavour apparently still considered the 'struggle against

Garibaldianism' to be his main task. ... Fundamentally the rift represented the natural division between Left and Right, between rashness and caution, radicalism and conservatism, between the method of the sword and the method of diplomacy. One side believed in all or nothing, while the other saw the value of circumlocution and gradualism. Yet both were necessary for the making of Italy.

From *Cavour and Garibaldi* by D. Mack Smith (1954)

Q Some Italian reviewers saw Mack Smith's work as an attack on Risorgimento heroes or even on Italians in general

It is not only that there is a prefabricated plan which represents a people perennially merry-making. There is something worse. ... He reduces the Risorgimento to a peaceful development through fortunate circumstances, to selfish interests, to a complex of material needs, to strokes of fortune and diplomatic deceit, to 'student escapades'; that is, he takes away its soul. The Risorgimento was spirit of sacrifice, it was suffering in the ways of exile and in the galleys, it was blood of Italian youth on the battlefields. ... It was the passion of a people for its Italian identity.

From a review of D. Mack Smith: *Italy: A Modern History* (1959) by N. Rodolico (1960)

R Mack Smith's work over 40 years has shed much light on the true nature of Italy's founders – even on the revered father of the nation, Victor Emmanuel II, whose archives are still protected by his heirs

Victor Emmanuel said that Italians could be governed only by bayonets or bribery, and hence could hardly live up to his public reputation of being a good and constitutional king. He showed more courage and occasionally more good judgement than his successors were to do, and he had a more attractive and forthright personality, yet equally he showed less sense of responsibility and less intelligent awareness of what he was doing. His passion for war, his incompetence as a military commander, his secret and thoroughly irresponsible opposition to his prime ministers ... were unfortunate aspects of his reign, particularly so in that he ruled at a time when, because traditions of Italian life were being formed, his contribution was the more obvious and consequential. Deliberately or by default, for good or ill, he probably did as much as Cavour to shape the political institutions and practice of united Italy.

From *Victor Emmanuel, Cavour and the Risorgimento* by D. Mack Smith (1971)

4 Recent views

In 1996 the journalist Matt Frei explained the political chaos of modern Italy by 'the basic failure of Italy to feel emotionally a united country'. The work of modern historians suggests a link between such alienation and the nature of the Risorgimento.

S Stuart Woolf draws attention to its narrow social base

Only some tens of thousands had participated as volunteers in the risings, movements and wars of the Risorgimento, and merely a few thousand had been involved actively in these movements as a 'political class'. ... It was hardly surprising, given its minute numbers and the manner in which it had imposed unity upon the country, that the moderate ruling class should have had an elitist attitude towards the problems of government and participation. ... Their cultural formation and the predominance of leaders from the north and centre explained their remoteness from the particular problems of the south, if not from the peasantry in general. Their remoteness was accentuated by the moderates' isolation even as a political class. The hostility of the Church, inevitable given the creation of the Italian state at the expense of the pope's temporal possessions ... deprived the moderates of the support of both priests and Catholic laity. Indeed, papal intransigence obliged the secular rulers to proclaim the authority of the state in assertive fashion through persistent fear of the deep and potentially subversive influence of the Church among the Italian people. The consequent brusqueness with which the 'legal' Italy imposed its power further isolated the moderates from the 'real', especially the rural, Italy.

From *A History of Italy 1700–1860: The Social Constraints of Political Change* by S. Woolf (1979)

T Lucy Riall makes a similar point

[Beneath the] political, diplomatic and economic disappointments of Italian unity ... [there] lay a deeper dissatisfaction with nationalism itself. ... National identity was defined very narrowly. Not only the poor and illiterate but all women, whose role in the Risorgimento was defined by Mazzini as that of 'mother, sister and wife', were excluded from legitimate participation in this new national public sphere.

From *The Italian Risorgimento* by L. Riall (1994)

The Making of Modern Italy

U The growth of Italian secessionist movements in the 1990s has raised further questions about the Risorgimento

Attention has shifted in the last five years from ideology to constitutional theory. It is no longer a question, principally, of establishing precisely how successful the liberal state was in achieving the social, economic and cultural goals which the various protagonists had anticipated, but rather of analysing the viability of the state itself. During the Risorgimento there was, in fact, a vigorous debate between unitarists and federalists which was largely disregarded once political unity was attained in 1861. This was a natural response of victors anxious to secure the spoils. ... Figures who had been centrally involved found that their roles had been all but written out of the grand narrative which legitimised the Italian state. Carlo Cattaneo, for example, was treated as an isolated eccentric. Yet he had been one of the principal leaders of the uprising in Milan in 1848 and the most authoritative commentator on the significance of that dramatic year. He was disregarded because he rejected the unitary state as an appropriate model for Italy and had little sympathy for the naive enthusiasms of orthodox nationalists. ... The force of federalist analyses of the Risorgimento has now been acknowledged. This has led to a much more positive view of the significance of the regions in modern Italian history. Where regional sentiment had once been seen as an outmoded attachment to tradition, it is now seen as a source of strength, enabling civil society to flourish in Italy despite weak and sometimes corrupt central administration and control.

From *Myth and Reality in the Risorgimento* by B. Haddock in *New Perspective*, December 1996

Questions

1 Analyse the faults and merits of Cavour or Mazzini or Garibaldi with reference to the relevant sources between A and I. **(6 marks)**
2 Demonstrate how sources J–N reveal the political opinions of their authors. **(8 marks)**
3 To what extent does source P justify the fears and criticisms voiced in sources O and Q? **(6 marks)**
4 Compare the ways in which Victor Emmanuel II is treated in sources G and R. **(4 marks)**
5 How do sources S–U suggest that Italy was not truly unified? **(6 marks)**

11 DEALING WITH EXAMINATION QUESTIONS

Specimen Answers to Source-based Questions

Questions based on Chapter 3 – 'Metternich and the Repression of Italy'
Questions

1 Explain the meaning of the following phrases as they are used in the sources:

   (a) 'geographical expression' (source A, line 2) **(2 marks)**
   (b) 'Italian jacobinism' (source A, line 10) **(2 marks)**
   (c) 'principles adopted by His Imperial Majesty for the internal government of his Italian provinces' (source B, lines 5–6) **(2 marks)**

2 What reliable information do sources D, E, G and Q give about the nature of Restoration governments in Italy? **(6 marks)**

3 How useful are sources C, F, H and I for finding out about the attitudes of Italian people in this period? **(6 marks)**

4 Assess the value of sources J–L and P for explaining the failure of Italian revolution in 1820–21 and 1831. **(6 marks)**

5 Which of sources L–O and R most vividly conveys the effects of repressive government during this period? **(6 marks)**

Points to note about these questions

1 To explain these phrases you may use the Introduction to Chapter 3 and your own knowledge of this period.

2 Here you will need to bear in mind the nature of the sources and their authors as well as what they say about the restored governments in Italy after the Treaty of Vienna.

The Making of Modern Italy

3 Care is needed in approaching this question as it is always difficult to find out about the attitudes of ordinary people, especially when dealing with a period when most of them were illiterate.

4 It is a good idea in answering this type of question to tackle the sources as a whole, judging to what extent they support each other and how complete a picture they give.

5 To decide which source gives you the strongest impression you must first compare them with each other.

Specimen answers

1 Explain the meaning of the following phrases as they are used in the sources:

(a) 'geographical expression' (source A, line 2) **(2 marks)**

In a phrase which was to go down in history Metternich makes it clear that, although geographically distinct, the Italian peninsula has no political identity as a whole. He scorns the whole idea of unification.

(b) 'Italian jacobinism' (source A, line 10) **(2 marks)**

Metternich is referring here to a minority of educated, middle-class Italians who adopted French Revolutionary ideas and often welcomed the French occupation of Italy in the late 1790s. They favoured constitutional government, religious toleration and the abolition of privilege. Some also hoped (vainly) that French rule might lead to a united Italy.

(c) 'principles adopted by His Imperial Majesty for the internal government of his Italian provinces' (Source B, lines 5–6) **(2 marks)**

This phrase in the secret treaty between Austria and the restored King of the Two Sicilies refers to the autocratic type of government by which Austria ruled Lombardy and Venetia. Metternich was anxious that there should be no revival of the constitutions introduced into Naples and Sicily by the French and British during the wars.

2 What reliable information do sources D, E, G and Q give about the nature of Restoration governments in Italy? **(6 marks)**

At the time of the Restoration, d'Azeglio was a young man whose family had had mixed experiences under Napoleonic rule. Like most Italians, d'Azeglio was glad to be rid of the French but, as an intelligent observer, he realised that it would be a mistake to throw out the beneficial changes they had brought. His account (source D) of the return to bigoted, reactionary methods accords well with Farini's description of Leo XII's rule in the Papal States (source G); both

Dealing with Examination Questions

suggest that practical programmes such as road-building and vaccinations came to an end while old forms of religious intolerance (including anti-semitism) returned. Although both accounts are by liberals, who clearly disliked the restored governments, their testimony is valuable. The list of repressive rules by which Austria ruled the Italians in its charge (source E) is a neutral source which backs up sources D and G, though we cannot tell how strictly the police observed these guidelines. The Memorandum from the Great Powers to the Pope (source Q) suggests that, in the Papal States at least, autocracy had not been relaxed by 1831.

3 How useful are sources C, F, H and I for finding out about the attitudes of Italian people in this period? **(6 marks)**

It is always more difficult to find out about the attitudes of ordinary people than about the behaviour of governments. If Metternich is to be believed (source C), the return of Austrian influence was welcomed by most Italian people and any opponents were too frightened to show their faces. Sources H and I are more direct evidence of both the conservative and the liberal wings of opinion. Here we see liberals joining secret societies (which suggests that they were indeed afraid to declare their views in public) and devout Catholics swearing to support the status quo. It is impossible to tell from these sources how widespread either type of organisation was, though we can glimpse the passion behind them. The effectiveness of the 'rod' which Metternich held over liberal Italians is revealed in source F. A well-meaning and apparently harmless journal is doomed to extinction, presumably because it dares to discuss the economic advance of Italy in general and to concern itself with 'principles of legislation' and 'institutions'. It is easy to imagine the frustration of *Il Conciliatore*'s editors and readers and that of educated Italians in other states where such censorship was practised. Taken together, these four sources suggest that Italian people had mixed and varied feelings about the restored governments.

4 Assess the value of sources J–L and P for explaining the failure of Italian revolution in 1820–21 and 1831. **(6 marks)**

Metternich's letters (source J) certainly reveal his own arrogance and contempt for the Italian people. But his determination to put an end to the 'Neapolitan event' and the 'Piedmontese affair', once the Austrians had recharged their 'fire-engines', also goes a long way towards explaining why these revolutions failed. His opinion that the rebels are divided and lack popular support may well arise partly from his own prejudice against the Italians; but it is borne out by d'Azeglio's sympathetic and detailed analysis of the Piedmontese revolution

The Making of Modern Italy

(source K). Even Mazzini has to admit that there was 'treachery' and 'weakness' among the rebels in 1821. The vague and over-optimistic declaration by Bolognese revolutionary leaders in 1831 (source P) unwittingly suggests that this too was 'an isolated effervescence' without a solid popular base. Together these four sources convincingly show that these poorly planned risings were no match for the Austrian army.

5 Which of sources L–O and R most vividly conveys the effects of repressive government during this period? **(6 marks)**

Sources L, O and R are all romantic evocations of suffering. Mazzini's youthful dedication of his life to the 'heroic struggle' (source L) is echoed by the inspiring print of Menotti's martyrdom (source R). Byron's account of the widespread arrest of dissidents is also highly-charged and emotional, idealising the Italian cause as a form of poetry. These three sources are vivid in capturing the spirit of the age but not in conveying what it was actually like to suffer at the hands of these repressive governments. That is done more effectively in Pellico's detailed description of the conditions he endured in an Austrian gaol (source M). But the plain drawing of Pellico's cell (source N) gives the strongest impression of the plight of Italian dissidents at this time.

Preparing Essay Answers

As reports of the examination boards point out year after year, the greatest single weakness among examinees is an inability to be relevant in their answers. No matter how well read and knowledgeable candidates may be, they cannot be given credit if they stray too far from the terms of the question. Examinations are a test of the ability to analyse historical material in such a way as to present a reasoned, informed response to a specific question. Too often examiners are faced with regurgitated notes, which do not relate much to the questions as set. Each question demands its own individual interpretation. The intelligence and subtlety of the candidates' responses will determine the marks they score.

Examinees must, of course, have knowledge, but academic history tests not only what they know but how well they use it. As an aid to effective examination technique, here is a list of questions that candidates should ask themselves when preparing essays:

1 *Have I answered the question* AS SET or have I simply imposed my prepared answer on it?

2 *Have I produced a genuine argument* or have I merely put down a

Dealing with Examination Questions

number of disconnected points in the hope that the examiners can work it out for themselves?

3 *Have I been relevant in arguing my case* or have I included ideas and facts that have no real relation to the question?

4 *Have I made appropriate use of primary or secondary sources to illustrate my answer?*

5 *Have I tried to show originality* or have I just played safe and written a safe answer?

Possible Essay Titles

1 What influence did the French Revolution and Napoleon have before 1815 on the Italian states?

Having given some idea of the huge upheaval wrought by the French in Europe between 1793 and 1815, this essay should consider their impact on Italy. The different stages of French rule should be outlined: the establishment of sister-republics based on French revolutionary principles and the creation of kingdoms to fit into Napoleon's imperial system. There are several controversial questions to discuss. To what extent were the French welcomed by Italian 'Jacobins'? How did most ordinary Italians feel about French taxes and conscription and about the treatment of the Pope? Did the whole experience indirectly strengthen Italian nationalism? Was it a different Italy to which the old rulers returned in 1815?

2 Why did Italy remain a 'geographical expression' during the period 1815–49?

This essay should identify and explain the various factors preventing unification before 1849. Internal divisions such as linguistic variation and regional particularism can be weighed against external forces like the hostility of the Great Powers (especially Austria). A paragraph could explain the different concepts of unity held by the few educated Italians who debated unification. Failure is well exemplified in the abortive risings of 1820–21, 1831 and 1848–9, though they should not be described in detail here. Mazzini's work in spreading propaganda and inspiring revolution typifies the brave but futile efforts of this period.

3 What were the lessons of 1848–9 for those interested in Italian liberation and unification? How well were they learned?

The Making of Modern Italy

The best way to answer this question is to link the two parts. Italian weakness in the face of Austrian military strength taught Cavour to plan carefully and to seek foreign help before attacking Austria again. He was also able to overcome the earlier problem of divided leadership by taking firm control of the movement, even managing to tame Garibaldi. The lack of popular support apparent in 1848–9 was tackled by the newly-formed National Society, as well as by Mazzini's continued propaganda. The events of 1859–61 should be used to judge how much nationalist leaders had learned from the mistakes of the past.

4 Why was so much of the progress towards Italian unification achieved in the years 1859 to 1861?

The key to this essay is to identify the factors which were present in 1859–61 but not earlier. The most decisive ones were the modernisation of Piedmont, Cavour's leadership, Napoleon III's interest in Italy and Garibaldi's decision to invade the South. It is also worth considering the work of the National Society and the new English Liberal party's sympathy with Italian nationalism. The limited nature of the Kingdom created in 1861 suggests that there were still inhibiting factors, such as the Pope's opposition, lukewarm popular support and Napoleon III's vacillations.

5 Examine the claim that Cavour ensured the freedom of Italy but Garibaldi ensured its unity.

These two concepts are obviously linked: there could be no unity without freedom because of Austria's domination of the peninsula. It could be argued that Cavour's priority was actually the enlargement of Piedmont, which was achieved by the expulsion of the Habsburgs from northern and central Italy. Cavour was probably prepared to settle for this amount of 'freedom', although he regretted the loss of Savoy and Nice and the exclusion of Venetia. Garibaldi was determined to unite the peninsula. His success in bringing Naples and Sicily into the kingdom was largely his own doing though all might have been lost had Cavour not prevented him from attacking Rome and incurring French wrath. Nationalists did not consider that an Italy without Rome and with a Piedmontese constitution was truly free or united. Thus there is no easy answer to this question – the quotation over-simplifies the issues.

6 Why, and in what ways, was the influence of other European countries important to the creation of a united Italy?

This essay covers a broad span. It could start by considering the

Dealing with Examination Questions

possible contribution of Napoleon I's conquests. After 1815 the strong presence of Austria in Italy made the Risorgimento an international question. Austria's crushing of early revolts, her partial defeat in 1859 and her expulsion from Venetia in 1866 should all be dealt with. But other countries were involved too. France helped to crush Italian nationalism in 1849 but fought to expel Austria in 1859; Napoleon III supported the Pope to the end in resisting the inclusion of Rome. The mixed motives for these policies should be examined. Prussia was indirectly involved in the later stages of unification, both by defeating Austria in 1866 and by causing the withdrawal of French troops from Rome in 1870. Britain's benevolent attitude was also important. Though the impetus came from Italians it is difficult to avoid the conclusion that their country was an international creation.

7 'The fate of Italy was decided by warfare and diplomacy rather than by national revival.' Discuss this statement.

This title requires similar subject matter to essay number 6; in addition to the warfare (in which relatively few Italian lives were lost) the complicated diplomacy behind the Plombières agreement of 1858 and the handing over of Venice in 1866 should be explained. But this question also invites some historiographical discussion of the old idea that Italy was created by a heroic national revival. It is relevant to point out occasions when nationalist feeling and effort were important: the defence of Rome in 1849, the successful revolts in central Italy in 1859 and the support for Garibaldi in 1860. Opinions still vary on which factors were more decisive.

8 In what ways was Italy still not fully unified by 1870?

A closer look at this rather surprising question suggests that the process of unification had itself created disunity. There were areas which nationalists continued to claim for Italy: Savoy and Nice (ceded to France) and the Tyrol ('unredeemed' from Austria). In the absence of any federal arrangements, many 'Italians' resented the domination of Piedmont and felt more loyal to their own regions. Under the Piedmontese constitution less than two per cent of the population could vote. Stark economic and social differences made a mockery of unity. This was especially true in the south where civil war had only just been quelled. The unresolved rift between Church and State made it hard for the Catholic flock to feel fully Italian. Some of these issues have been settled over the years but as the millennium approaches separatist feeling in Italy remains strong.

The Making of Modern Italy

Specimen Essay Answer

(See especially Chapters 4, 5 and 10)
Examine Mazzini's contribution to making Italy 'independent, united and free'.

'Cavour made Italy', wrote the *Spectator* in its obituary of Mazzini in 1872. This is often stated, but less frequently added is the qualification that 'it was due to Mazzini, not Cavour, that such making was possible'. This essay examines the truth of the second part of the statement.

Mazzini's 'irrevocable determination' to free Italy began when he encountered rebels fleeing from Piedmont in 1821. He joined the *Carbonari*, one of the few revolutionary organisations available at that time, but did not approve of its secret methods. After a spell in prison he left Italy and at Marseilles established Young Italy, a 'brotherhood of Italians' who would openly strive through 'education and insurrection' for an independent, united republic. Hunted by the agents of Metternich, who called him 'the most dangerous man in Europe', Mazzini found refuge in England where he was to live for most of his life.

From a secret address in London he conducted a propaganda campaign designed to educate public opinion. He sent thousands of letters, pamphlets and newspapers to Italy, where most were read only by Italian or Austrian censors. It is difficult to judge whether the material that got through had much effect – after all, as Mazzini himself said, 'the people cannot read'. Nevertheless he probably helped to spread the idea of a united Italy among educated Italians, even if his democratic republic did not find as much favour as Gioberti's proposal for a federation of states led by the Pope.

Mazzini's efforts, as well as such money as he could raise, were also devoted to organising insurrections, which he justified with the argument that there was no other way of breaking free from the 'vast prison' of Italy. The failure of these ventures is only too obvious; the Bandiera brothers, for instance, were arrested and shot as soon as they set foot in Calabria in 1844.

The time when Mazzini's ideas came closest to fruition was in 1848–9. His hopes were raised by the liberalism of the new Pope, Pius IX, and by Charles Albert's early success in his war against Austria. He returned to Italy where he was greeted enthusiastically wherever he went. When, in February 1849, a Republic was declared in Rome, Mazzini's dreams seemed close to realisation. The support he enjoyed at this point is shown by his election as the Republic's leader. By all accounts he ruled wisely and moderately during its short life, belying fears that he was a godless follower of Karl Marx. Nevertheless, other parts of Italy refused his invitation to unite with Rome. In fact, the King of Naples answered instead the Pope's call for help and sent troops to help the forces of France crush the Republic. Its brave defence by Garibaldi's volunteers saved nothing except Italian honour. But it also created a legend which helped to inspire the Risorgimento.

Back in exile, Mazzini resumed his old activities. He directed a disastrous Milanese rising in 1853 and in 1857 encouraged Carlo Pisacane to take a band of revolutionaries to Naples, where they were soon killed. Not surprisingly, many former Mazzinians concluded that Italy was not ready for revolution and supported the National Society which had been founded in Turin. Its members, who included Garibaldi, shared Mazzini's aim of creating an independent and united Italy; but they rejected revolution and accepted the leadership of the Piedmontese monarchy.

The new Prime Minister of Piedmont was the cunning pragmatist, Count Cavour, who abhorred all that Mazzini stood for. Yet Cavour was prepared, as in 1857, to turn a blind eye to revolutionary plotting when his own devious schemes required evidence that Italians were eager to be liberated. In fact Cavour was probably behind Orsini's attempt to assassinate Napoleon III in 1858. The Prime Minister was able to use this incident to persuade the French Emperor to fight for Italy's independence from Austria. By June 1859 Austria had been expelled from Lombardy.

It seems that Cavour's methods had been proved successful. But it is hard to estimate the extent to which the simultaneous revolts in Tuscany, Parma, Modena and Romagna resulted from Mazzini's long propaganda campaign and from his presence in Italy at that time. To the radicals' dismay, Cavour and the National Society now took charge in these areas and organised plebiscites which confirmed the union with Piedmont. Mazzini did not join in the rejoicing when over a third of Italy was united into one kingdom. Nor did Garibaldi, who denounced the 'sale' of Nice and Savoy 'to the foreigner'. The two nationalists now resumed their friendship and dedicated themselves to the full unification of Italy.

For ten years Mazzini had been urging Garibaldi to lead an expedition to Sicily. In 1860 both the patriot-soldier's state of mind and conditions in Sicily (where Mazzini's agents had stirred up revolt) made the venture feasible. Garibaldi's startling success in Sicily and Naples, which was largely due to the widespread support he commanded, was a triumph for Mazzini's ideal of liberty won through a popular movement. Furthermore, Mazzini planned to incite revolution in the Papal States, which prompted Cavour and Victor Emmanuel to forestall the 'red republicans' by taking over those areas themselves.

The Making of Modern Italy

Thus, as Denis Mack Smith writes, 'the revolutionaries had the satisfaction of knowing that they had provoked another major step towards unification'. So, although it was not the ideal outcome he had dreamed of, the Italian Kingdom formed in 1861 was partly Mazzini's creation. But he himself was still under sentence of death and once again he had to flee his native land.

In his later years Mazzini continued both his propaganda and his conspiracies, directed still towards the declaration of a republic and also towards the acquisition of Venice and Rome. As late as 1870 he was arrested and imprisoned, during an attempt to organise a new Sicilian rising. He was infuriated by the humiliating and furtive way in which Venice and Rome were gained in 1866 and 1870. In a final verdict Mazzini denounced Italy as 'a living lie'. In his opinion a country created by the 'calculating dynastic egoism of foreigners', lacking vital indigenous areas and without a republican constitution was *not* 'independent, united and free'. But this view hardly does full justice to the great achievement of uniting Italy, to which Mazzini had made an unparalleled contribution.

BIBLIOGRAPHY

An interesting way to study the Unification of Italy is to visit the Risorgimento museums in Italian cities, all of which have a different regional bias. Particularly recommended are those in Turin (where Charles Albert is a hero), Genoa (housed in Mazzini's family home), Venice (a shrine to Daniele Manin) and Milan. Rome's Museum of the Risorgimento has been unaccountably closed for years. It is also worth listening to Verdi's operas, especially *Macbeth* and *Nabucco*. The following list contains some of the primary and secondary material written in or translated into English. The references in the text also give suggestions for further reading.

R. Absalom: *Italy Since 1800* (Longman 1995). A recent history which encompasses present-day Italy.

G. Abba: *Diary of One of Garibaldi's Thousand*, trans. E. R. Vincent (OUP 1962). A fascinating first-hand account of Garibaldi's campaign.

D. Beales: *The Risorgimento and the Unification of Italy* (Longman 1981). An informative introduction followed by a selection of substantial documents.

A. Boime: *The Art of the Macchia and the Risorgimento* (University of Chicago 1993). An exploration of the links between Italian artists and the politics of the period.

Lord Byron: *Selected Letters and Journals* (Penguin 1984). An English Romantic's view of Italian struggles in the 1820s.

M. d'Azeglio: *Things I Remember*, trans. E. R. Vincent (OUP 1966). The memoirs of an important Piedmontese artist and politician.

G. di Lampedusa: *The Leopard*, trans. A. Colquoun (Harvill Press 1996). An evocative novel by a Sicilian nobleman about the death throes of feudal Sicily.

C. Dickens: *Pictures from Italy* (OUP 1957). The great writer's affectionate impressions of Italy in the 1840s.

P. Ginsborg: *Daniele Manin and the Venetian Revolution of 1848–9* (CUP 1979). A masterly account of this troubled time in Venice.

E. E. Y. Hales: *Pio Nono* (Eyre & Spottiswoode 1954). A sympathetic but fair biography by a Catholic historian.

H. Hearder: *Cavour* (Historical Association 1972). A concise summary of Cavour's achievements.

H. Hearder: *Italy in the Age of the Risorgimento 1790–1870* (Longman 1983). A broad-ranging survey which pays particular attention to regional diversity and to the culture of nineteenth-century Italy.

C. Hibbert: *Garibaldi and His Enemies* (Penguin 1987). A readable account of Garibaldi's eventful life.

M. Lutyens: *Effie in Venice* (John Murray 1965). A collection of Effie Ruskin's letters which gives a fascinating glimpse of Venice.

D. Mack Smith: *The Making of Italy* (Harper Torchbooks 1968). A valuable collection of authoritative original sources.

D. Mack Smith: *Victor Emmanuel, Cavour and the Risorgimento* (CUP 1971). A series of illuminating essays.

D. Mack Smith: *Garibaldi: A Portrait in Documents* (Passigli Edition 1982). An attractive book containing many visual sources.

D. Mack Smith: *Cavour* (Weidenfeld & Nicholson 1985) and *Mazzini* (Yale University Press 1994). Elegantly-written biographies of these important political figures.

A. Manzoni: *The Betrothed*, trans. A. Colquoun (Dent 1952). The first novel written in Italian, still widely read by Italians.

S. Pellico: *My Prisons*, trans. G. Lapaldi (OUP 1963). A moving book which was very influential in its time.

L. Riall: *The Italian Risorgimento* (Routledge 1994). A social and political survey taking account of the most recent research.

Stendhal: *The Charterhouse of Parma* (Penguin 1958). An exciting novel set in the Napoleonic wars.

W. G. Shreeves: *Nationmaking in Nineteenth-Century Europe* (Nelson 1954). A thematic treatment of Italian and German unification.

A. Stiles: *The Unification of Italy* (Hodder & Stoughton 1986). A useful examination of the issues written for A-level students.

G. M. Trevelyan: *Garibaldi and the Making of Italy* (Longman 1911). An interesting example of the great liberal historian's work.

S. Woolf: *The Italian Risorgimento* (Longman 1959). A wide-ranging collection of primary and secondary sources.

S. Woolf: *A History of Italy 1700–1860: Social Constraints of Political Change* (Methuen 1979). As the subtitle suggests, a vital new emphasis on the Italian people during the Risorgimento.

INDEX

Abba, Guiseppe 94–6, 137
Alfieri, Vittorio 7–9, 16

Balbo, Cesare 5, 42–3, 54
Bismarck, Otto von 4, 104–6
Byron, Lord 38, 130, 137

Carbonari 29–30, 34–5, 37, 134
Cattaneo, Carlo 43, 50–1, 55, 63, 126
Cavour, Camillo 3–6, 52, 67–70, 72, 74–84, 87, 90–4, 96–7, 100, 102–5, 108–10, 113, 117–18, 122–4, 126, 132, 134–5, 137–8
Charles Albert (King of Piedmont) 2–3, 5, 31, 43, 52, 54–7, 59–60, 66, 134, 137

D'Azeglio, Massimo 27, 33, 36, 42, 47, 52, 54, 67–8, 117, 128–9, 137

Ferdinand I (King of Naples) 8, 18, 29–30, 32, 54–7

Garibaldi, Guiseppe 3–4, 6, 42, 57, 68, 81, 90–106, 108, 112, 115, 120–4, 126, 132–3, 135, 137
Gioberti, Vincenzo 5, 41–2, 46, 56, 67, 72, 78
Gladstone, William 34, 70–1, 81
Gregorovius, Ferdinand 106–7, 110–11, 113–15

Jacobins 17–19, 24, 131
Jews 18, 29, 34

La Farina, Guiseppe 68, 92, 96–7

Manin, Daniele 55–6, 62–3, 68, 76, 78, 137
Manzoni, Alessandro 5, 12, 25–6, 42, 48, 138
Mazzini, Guiseppe 2–5, 31–2, 36, 41–6, 48, 52–4, 56–7, 65–6, 68–9, 76, 80–1, 90–1, 93, 97, 104, 116, 118–20, 122, 126, 130–2, 134–8
Menotti, Ciro 31–2, 39, 130
Metternich, Prince 29–32, 35, 54–5, 127–9, 134
Murat, Marshal 4, 19–20, 25, 29, 35

Napoleon I 2, 4, 17–20, 22–30, 33, 131, 133
Napoleon III (Louis Napoleon) 3, 5–6, 56, 69, 77–81, 83, 86–7, 90, 92, 102, 104–6, 114–15, 132–3, 135
National Society 5, 68, 76, 80, 132, 135
Nelson, Admiral 18–19, 24
Nigra, Costantino 83, 94, 97, 109

Orsini, Felice 5, 69, 77, 135

Pallavicino, Giorgio 68, 76
Palmerston, Lord 43, 53, 63–4, 81
Pellico, Silvio 5, 31, 37–8, 41, 130, 138
Pisacane, Carlo 5, 57, 66, 68–9, 76, 135
Pius IX, Pope 2, 4–6, 43, 54–7, 62–3, 66–7, 81, 86, 89, 102, 104–7, 110–11, 114–15, 117, 137

Radetzky, Marshal 55–6, 61–2, 67
Ratazzi, Urbano 102, 105–6
Russell, Lord John 81, 86–7, 89, 92, 104, 108, 111, 114–15

Settembrini, Luigi 13, 57–8, 64–5, 71

Verdi, Guiseppe 5, 42–3, 48, 88, 137
Victor Emmanuel I (King of Piedmont) 29, 31–2
Victor Emmanuel II (King of Italy) 3–6, 57, 67, 69, 72–3, 77, 79–81, 84, 87–9, 92–3, 97, 101, 103–7, 110, 113, 115, 119, 122, 124, 126, 138
Victoria, Queen 72–3, 79, 82

GLOSSARY OF FOREIGN TERMS

ancien régime	old (pre-revolutionary) ways of ruling
Carbonari	(literally charcoal burners) secret societies set up to oppose Napoleon and subsequently the restored autocratic rulers
farà da sé	the idea that Italy should unite itself without foreign help
fascism	totalitarian form of government established in Italy by Mussolini after 1922
ghetto	area in which Jews are forced to live
incognito	secretly and anonymously
Italia Una	United Italy
latifundia	large estates
lazzari	urban workers
Marseillaise	French Revolutionary anthem
piazza	town square
Pio Nono	Pope Pius IX
Re	King
Renaissance	period of great artistic and cultural achievement which began in fifteenth-century Italy
risorgimento	national revival of Italy
Risorgimento	the period of Italy's unification
sanfedisti	conservative Catholic secret societies
statuto	constitution
trattoria	ordinary restaurant
tricolour	green, white and red flag of Italy or blue, white and red flag of France
Viva!	long live!